ICNC **MONOGRAPH** SERIES

Resource Mobilization in Palestinian Nonviolent Campaigns

Mahmoud Soliman

ICNC
PRESS

Contents

Chapter 6. Leveraging Short-Term and Long-Term Opportunities
for Acquiring or Harnessing Resources

Chapter 7. Managing Material and Non-material Resources

Tables and Figures

EXECUTIVE SUMMARY

This monograph analyzes how Palestinian grassroots activists, popular resistance committees (PRCs), and popular resistance networks (PRNs) secured, managed, and used material and non-material resources to wage sustained and successful nonviolent campaigns in Area C of the occupied West Bank.

The study develops a comprehensive analytical framework to capture a variety of material and non-material resources and better understand the role that different types of resources play in the launching, conducting, and outcomes of a nonviolent campaign.

The in-depth cases consist of three nonviolent campaigns led by Palestinian communities living under full Israeli military occupation. Harsh conditions have been bearing on poor communication infrastructure, economic hardship, and low technical skills among Palestinians. And yet, Palestinian activists managed to secure, administer, and deploy a diverse range of material and non-material resources to launch, conduct, and sustain their campaigns and achieve their goals.

This monograph offers lessons to campaign organizers on how to acquire and harness resources and illustrates how acquisition of one type of resource helps secure other resources. It examines the mechanisms that campaigns developed to manage and deploy different kinds of resources by successfully involving affected residents in campaign decision-making processes and by addressing actual community problems identified through organic need-assessment processes. This approach ensured the legitimacy of the campaigns in the eyes of the local communities and, in turn, mobilized further participation.

This monograph finds that there are limitations on the effective mobilization of resources when organizational structure, skills, and communication mechanisms are missing or are in short supply. It also shows that non-monetary material resources have greater positive impact on campaigns than financial resources secured from external actors. Non-monetary and non-material resources played a key role in sustaining activism, strengthening nonviolent discipline, and increasing residents' participation in the campaigns. This study also finds that the best strategy to overcome the challenges posed by internal division and the imposition of external agendas is to maintain the independence of the campaign, keep leadership in the hands of local activists, and prioritize the needs of communities over political affiliates. This strategy has prevented local campaigns from being co-opted by outside actors. Finally, resources that were harnessed internally—directly from the communities involved—have generally proven more beneficial to the campaigns than externally sourced financial contributions. Their use was also less constrained by bureaucratic and reporting requirements imposed by domestic and international donors.

In its conclusion, this study offers specific recommendations and lessons learned from the investigated cases for various actors, including activists, allies that want to support grass-roots campaigns, and researchers interested in furthering the study of the role and impact of resources in nonviolent organizing and their successful acquisition by local organizers.

Glossary of Acronyms

AP	**Assopace Palestina**
ARIJ	The Applied Research Institute Jerusalem
AFPS	**Association France Palestine Solidarité**
CPT	Christian Peacemaker Teams
EAPPI	**Ecumenical Accompaniment Program in Palestine and Israel**
EU	European Union
INGO	**International Non-Governmental Organization**
ISM	International Solidarity Movement
JV	**Jordan Valley**
JVS	Jordan Valley Solidarity
NGO	**Non-Governmental Organization**
Novact	International Institute for Nonviolent Action
NVR	**Nonviolent Resistance**
OPT	Occupied Palestinian Territories
PLO	**Palestinian Liberation Organization**
PM	Prime Minister
PNA	**Palestinian National Authority**
PRC	Popular Resistance Committee
PRN	**Popular Resistance Network**
PSCC	Popular Struggle Coordination Committee
RV	**Rebuilding Villages**
SCI	Service Civil International
SHH	**South Hebron Hills**
UN	United Nations

Chapter 1. Setting the Analytical Framework Straight

This monograph studies the Palestinian popular resistance campaigns that are taking place in Area C, which is the portion of the West Bank under full Israeli military occupation. It focuses on the ways that material and non-material resources have been generated by Palestinian campaigns in the South Hebron Hills (SHH), the Jordan Valley (the Jordan Valley Solidarity campaign, or JVS), and the Rebuilding Villages (RV) campaign across the Occupied Palestinian Territories (OPT). The study looks at the types of material and non-material resources that have been harnessed by domestic actors and acquired from external sources for use in nonviolent campaigns. It also examines the mechanisms developed by Palestinian grassroots organizations to manage and deploy these resources to carry out local campaigns.

In this study, the term "popular resistance" denotes Palestinian efforts to contest the Israeli occupation. This is a widely used term in Palestine that carries implications unique to the Palestinians' protracted anti-occupation struggle and that captures the full range of non-violent resistance actions. Popular resistance in Palestine is not rooted in principled nonviolence driven by a moral, ethical, or religious commitment to avoid violence. Nor does it directly condemn violence. Instead, Palestinian popular resistance can be characterized as an anti-occupation resistance, without the use of arms, that allows everyone to participate according to their ability through simple and nonviolent tactics without them necessarily having to condemn or reject the right to armed resistance in self-defense.

Popular resistance is understood as an individual and collective refusal to accept the status quo—expressed through protests, civil disobedience, and other acts of noncooperation and the constructive resistance of institution-building—with the aim of placing coercive, though nonviolent, pressure on the Israeli authorities. This monograph demonstrates that popular resistance in the Palestinian context comprises evolving tactics. However, for ease of reference, the terms popular resistance, nonviolent resistance, unarmed resistance, and civil resistance will be used interchangeably throughout because they all describe the nature of resistance used in the OPT.

Drawing on detailed interviews with activists, this study seeks to identify how the tactics used by Palestinian popular resistance committees (PRCs) and popular resistance networks (PRNs) have generated resources. It also identifies the organizational skills that these groups used to acquire and manage different kinds of material resources in support of various non-violent campaigns.

During the fieldwork research, the author had a dual role as researcher and activist. He has been organizing and participating in popular resistance campaigns since 2005 and has personally witnessed how local activists in the three campaigns generated resources. As an activist, the author has been in charge of using and managing material resources, particularly in the campaigns to rebuild houses demolished by the occupier in the SHH.

Through the author's involvement in all of the stages of popular resistance campaigns—from their planning to execution—he has witnessed their unity, their achievements, and their growth and spread across the OPT. The concerns about the issue of resources that are expressed in this monograph arise out of the author's first-hand encounters with the problems, challenges, and opportunities resources create.

Since 1948, resistance in rural Palestine has often operated at the personal and community levels, and material and non-material resources have helped improve campaigns' effectiveness and cohesion. Resources in this monograph are defined as assets, skills, or forms of support that are acquired or, in some cases, are available but dormant in the community until they are strategically harnessed and deployed by activists to advance campaign's goals.

In this study, the term "resources" refers to all available and acquired assets that campaign actors can use to achieve campaign goals. Resources can range from publicly expressed support and solidarity for a campaign to skills, knowledge, experience, money, time, materials, and people. In the simplest terms, as Ganz (2000) explained, resources are things that can be used to achieve something else.

Through the empirical analysis of three Palestinian campaigns, this study provides refined theoretical and practical insights into the types, nature, role, and impact of resources. It also demonstrates how specific nonviolent campaigns generated different kinds of resources to advance their demands and goals.

Analytical Framework: Material and Non-material Resources

This monograph employs a basic framework which allows us to analyze the acquisition, management, use, and impact of resources in the specific case studies included in this monograph.[1] Within this framework, resources are categorized as either material or non-material. Material resources are tangible assets of all kinds that can be used to implement campaign actions or secure and increase additional resources. Non-material resources are intangible resources,

---

1   This framework is constructed and adapted from the work of numerous scholars, including Edwards and McCarthy 2004; Gamson, et al. 1982; Cress and Snow 1996; Zald and Jacobs 1978; Knoke 1986; Oliver and Marwell 1992; Verba, et al. 1995; Hutchison 2012; and Lahusen 1996. It has also been heavily informed and refined by this study's empirical findings about the conduct of Palestinian nonviolent campaigns.

but they can also be used to recruit or deploy material resources (see Table 1). Both material and non-material resources are here defined.

To illustrate these definitions, different types of resources with corresponding examples are identified and categorized as either material or non-material resources. Interconnections between different resources are also explored, in situations where, for example, one type generates other types.

Table 1. Material vs. Non-material Resources

Material Resources	All kinds of tangible assets that can be used to implement campaign actions or secure and increase other resources. They enable a campaign to operate even under severe repression. Material resources include financial, in-kind contributions, building materials and equipment, and human and organizational resources.
Non-material Resources	All kinds of intangible resources that can be used to recruit or deploy material resources. Non-material resources include social and cultural resources that comprise social capital.

Material Resources

Material resources are divided between monetary resources, which include financial contributions and proceeds, and non-monetary resources, which include in-kind contributions, human and organizational resources, and building materials and equipment, as shown in Table 2.

Table 2. Categorization of Material Resources

MATERIAL RESOURCES			
MONETARY RESOURCES	NON-MONETARY RESOURCES		
FINANCIAL CONTRIBUTIONS AND PROCEEDS	IN-KIND CONTRIBUTIONS	HUMAN AND ORGANIZATIONAL RESOURCES	BUILDING MATERIALS AND EQUIPMENT
• Monetary donations • Grants • Sale of goods and services	• Food and drinks • Rooms • Printing services • Means of transportation, including cars, horses, and donkeys	• Volunteer labor • Construction skills • Skills in media communication and documentation • Local organizational networks • Transnational networks with established NGOs	• Bricks, sand, iron, gravel, cement, and basecourse (foundations for roads) • Bolster, hammers, hoes, hoists, spades, water levels, shovels, ladders, masonry, trowels, pickaxes, wheelbarrows • Infrastructural equipment, including solar panels and plastic pipelines

The primary **financial resources** used in the three campaigns is money generated from contributions (donations and grants) and proceeds from the sale of local goods and services, which help cover the expenses of campaign operations.

In-kind contributions are non-monetary contributions of goods and services from residents and include food and drinks for volunteers, rooms used for holding campaign meetings, printing services, and different means of transportation—from cars to animals—that are made available for a campaign.

Human and organizational resources are the people who join the campaigns and the specific organizational skills and networks they bring into their activism. More specifically, these resources include volunteer labor, construction skills, media communication and documentation skills, and local organizational and transnational networks:

- **Volunteer labor** is the involvement of residents from the communities who have the time and ability to volunteer for campaign activities, such as helping to renovate caves and water wells, construct buildings by making concrete or building bricks, and dig soil to install plastic water pipelines.

- **Construction skills** include the ability to build bricks, plaster walls, install doors, windows, and tin roofs.

- **Media communication and documentation skills** include writing reports, operating cameras, and conducting interviews. Local activists attended different training sessions to gain and hone their skills in the effective use of cameras to document actions. They were taught how to write concise media reports, how to give short interviews to journalists and how to document house demolitions by the Israeli military and Israeli settlers. These trainings were offered to the campaign activists by PRNs (such as the PSCC) and Israeli human rights and solidarity organizations (such as B'Tselem and ISM).

- **Local organizational networks** include Palestinian groups, networks, and NGOs.

- **Transnational networks** are external solidarity groups, including nongovernmental organizations outside of Palestine.

Building materials and equipment are non-monetary resources used by locals in their construction campaigns. Building materials range from bricks, sand, and iron, to gravel, base-course, and cement. Equipment includes tools required to construct housing and essential infrastructure such as bolster, hammers, hoes, hoists, spades, water levels, shovels, ladders, masonry, trowels, pickaxes, concrete mixers, and wheelbarrows.

Connections Between Material Resources

The case studies demonstrate interesting interactions between individual types of material resources. Figure 1, on the next page, highlights how certain material resources generate other material resources. Human and organizational resources are a necessity in the early stages of a campaign as they help generate in-kind contributions, financial resources, and building materials. Local networks allow for the recruitment of additional volunteers and the acquisition of in-kind contributions and financial resources, while volunteer labor and skills convert building and infrastructure materials into campaign products, such as newly built houses or habitable caves.

In-kind contributions are also important in the early stages when campaign actors have not yet built their external networks. They help move a campaign forward by providing a space for human, financial, and building materials to be effectively acquired and deployed.

Financial resources also help generate human and organizational resources, in-kind contributions, and building materials and equipment. In the case studies discussed in this monograph, effectively deploying other kinds of material resources culminated in the availability of building materials and equipment. For example, activists secured bricks, cement, and sand as a result of acquiring grants and financial contributions.

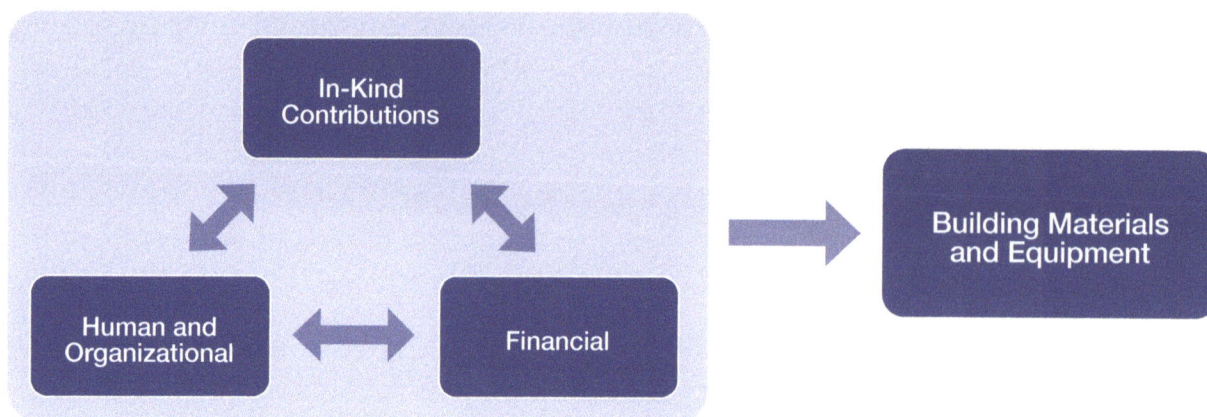

FIGURE 1. Interaction Among the Different Types of Material Resources

Non-material Resources

The non-material resources discussed in this study comprise the social capital existing in Palestinian semi-Bedouin communities, which played an important role in helping campaigns acquire resources. The semi-Bedouins are ethnically Palestinian, nomadic, and tribal communities that gradually settled in areas in the South Hebron Hills (SHH) and the Jordan Valley (JV) where they supplemented their herding activities with agricultural practices, transforming from a Bedouin to a semi-Bedouin lifestyle as a consequence. In practice, their nomadism ceased largely due to the occupation's restrictions. These communities are characterized by their communal loyalty, their strong sense of belonging to the land, hospitality, willingness to sacrifice for the tribe, and their patient and simple life—they enrich Palestinian society with their traditions, norms, and productivity. The characteristics of such communities mean that they have been able to contribute rich non-material resources to the campaigns in the form of both social and cultural resources (see Table 3).

Table 3. Types of Non-material Resources

NON-MATERIAL RESOURCES (SOCIAL CAPITAL)	
SOCIAL RESOURCES	**CULTURAL RESOURCES**

• Family relations
• Neighborhood acquaintances
• Communal trust
• Social networks
	• Semi-Bedouin tradition and faith
	• Palestinian cultural norms and values:
	  • *Onah*
	  • *Sumud*
	  • *Ma'dood*
	• Local knowledge:
	  • Legal knowledge
	  • Technical knowledge

Social resources include family relations, neighborhood acquaintanceships, informal social networks between local people, and communal trust. **Cultural resources** include semi-Bedouin traditions and local knowledge gained by the residents.

The cultural resources of **Semi-Bedouin tradition and faith** are intertwined with one another. Since the early stages of Islam, there was a harmonious coexistence between semi-Bedouin tradition and Islamic norms. Generosity, hospitality, prioritizing community interest over personal interest and a simple lifestyle close to the nature are all part of Bedouin tradition but are also key Islamic tenants. Donations and financial contributions—an important part of the Islamic culture—have played a key role in the philanthropic actions of the residents of the SHH and JV communities in support of local campaigns.

Palestinian cultural norms and values include *Onah, Ma'dood*, and *Sumud:*

- *Onah* is an old, traditional countryside practice used by Palestinians—including semi-Bedouin communities—according to which people offer each other help building houses and harvesting crops. It fosters mutual solidarity and voluntary work for the benefit of family members, neighbors, and local communities as a whole. According to one activist farmer, "You cannot rest while your neighbor did not finish his harvest."[2] The mutual aid that is ingrained in *Onah* becomes a moral duty when someone in the community is in distress, as one elderly man interviewed for this study noted: "I went with my sons and grandsons to help our neighbor rebuild his home which was demolished by the army. It would have been shameful if we did not help them."[3]

- *Ma'dood* is another tradition which is used as a non-material resource to generate financial contributions from family members. It is a tradition whereby community members are each obligated to contribute financial support toward public services through financial contributions to the project committees.

- Another local practice and philosophy that plays an important role in the longevity of resistance is *Sumud* (or steadfastness). *Sumud* is a form of everyday resistance—widely understood in Palestinian communities—that proactively keeps alive the spirit of defiance toward the occupier and promotes inner peace, self-confidence, and love for others.[4] *Sumud* enables many people to engage in individual actions that cumulatively produce a resistance force that can bring about change on the ground, even in the most repressive contexts or in the face of insurmountable obstacles.

---

2   Interview with an activist farmer from the north of the Jordan Valley, 18 June 2019.

3   Interview with an elderly farmer from the north of the Jordan Valley, 18 June 2019.

4   See Teeffelen 2011; Richter 2011; and Ryan 2015.

The words of an Al Mufaqara community member interviewed for this study capture well the meaning of *Sumud* as understood by the locals:

We are eight big families in this village. We have been here for a long time. Our ancestors lived here, and we succeeded them. We stayed here, we suffered and experienced hardship because of the occupation. The occupation expelled us to Al Tuwani village. They threw away our belongings, they dispersed us, but we survived, and we turned out to be stronger than them. We sued them and did not wither until we reached the Israeli Supreme Court. We won the support of international and Israeli activists. But even after we were able to return to our village, the occupation continued oppressing us. They failed to expel us the first time, so they kept trying again. They poisoned our cattle so that we would lose hope and leave the village. But we stayed! Despite the loss of the cattle and the suffering of the children, we stayed! We did not leave! We were born here, and we have to stay here. We kept on the traditions of our ancestors.[5]

The cultural resource of **local knowledge**, in turn, includes legal knowledge and expertise, and technical knowledge, that is, an understanding of the Israeli army's repression tactics, in-depth resistance experience, and local know-how such as agricultural knowledge:

- **Legal knowledge** is the knowledge about legal ecosystem in which activists operate. This concerns domestic, Israeli, and international legal aspects relevant to the context of the occupation, including responsibilities of the occupying power in the light of international law. Residents gained this knowledge through their interactions with the Israeli activists and lawyers. The PRNs established an educational program on international law and popular resistance while some NGOs and INGOs conducted workshops focused specifically on international law and the rights of Palestinians.

- **Technical knowledge** is the knowledge that residents have gained through their living experience in their own communities and includes the knowledge of the type of soil in the area that is essential to construct houses, dig caves or water wells, or knowledge of how to use traditional methods to build or renovate caves or existing water wells. Technical knowledge also includes agricultural knowledge. JV and SHH residents cultivate their land through traditional agricultural methods. Their skills in sustaining the land and their agricultural methods—including planting and harvesting the crops with simple tools—have been helpful for residents to maintain their presence on the land despite occupation and to bypass the Israeli restrictions. In the areas with limited access, residents have planted olive trees, as they need little upkeep. Furthermore, technical knowledge includes the understanding of how the Israeli army operates on

---

5   Interview with an elderly woman from one of the hamlets of SHH. Al Mufaqara, 10 June 2019.

a daily basis. People who are subject to an occupation acquire a deep knowledge of the occupier's operations, and thus are able to use this knowledge to their benefit in their anti-occupation struggle.

In the absence of material resources, social capital plays an enabling role that helps communities to launch effective campaigns. It is a facilitating factor that enables activists to harness material resources. In other words, non-material resources are often used to recruit or deploy material resources to meet campaign's goals (see Figure 2).

FIGURE 2. Material and Non-material Resources

Figure 2 illustrates the interaction between non-material and material resources, the predominant relationship being that non-material resources are harnessed and deployed to acquire material resources. For instance, non-material resources such as family relations and traditions helped generate building materials and equipment, as well as financial resources.

The full spectrum of resources presented and discussed in this study is listed in Table 4, on the next page.

Table 4. Spectrum of Material and Non-material Resources and Their Types

MATERIAL RESOURCES			
MONETARY RESOURCES	NON-MONETARY RESOURCES		
FINANCIAL CONTRIBUTIONS AND PROCEEDS	IN-KIND CONTRIBUTIONS	HUMAN AND ORGANIZATIONAL RESOURCES	BUILDING MATERIALS AND EQUIPMENT
• Monetary donations • Grants • Sale of goods and services	• Food and drinks • Rooms • Printing services • Means of transportation, including cars, horses, and donkeys	• Volunteer labor • Construction skills • Skills in media communication and documentation • Local organizational networks • Transnational networks with established NGOs	• Bricks, sand, iron, gravel, cement, and basecourse (foundations for roads) • Bolster, hammers, hoes, hoists, spades, water levels, shovels, ladders, masonry, trowels, pickaxes, wheelbarrows • Infrastructural equipment, including solar panels and plastic pipelines

NON-MATERIAL RESOURCES
(SOCIAL CAPITAL)

SOCIAL RESOURCES	CULTURAL RESOURCES

• Family relations
• Neighborhood acquaintances
• Communal trust
• Social networks
	• Semi-Bedouin tradition and faith
	• Palestinian cultural norms and values:
	  • *Onah*
	  • *Sumud*
	  • *Ma'dood*
	• Local knowledge:
	  • Legal knowledge
	  • Technical knowledge

Analytical Framework: Domestic and External Actors

This study's framework for assessing resources is complemented by a framework for assessing the actors involved in campaigns. Actors are categorized as either domestic actors or external actors.

Domestic actors are those residing in the OPT. They might be connected to or affected by the campaigns, regardless of their involvement in campaign actions. Domestic actors are further categorized as community residents, members of community organizations such as popular resistance committees (PRCs) and popular resistance networks (PRNs), or the Palestinian National Authority (PNA), which is the interim self-government body established as a consequence of the 1993–95 Oslo Accords. The PNA exercises partial civil control over the Gaza Strip and Areas A and B in the West Bank. Domestic actors can be members of more than one of these categories. **Campaign members** are the domestic actors, from any subcategory, who are directly involved in campaign actions.

PRCs and PRNs are grassroots umbrella organizations and networks that encourage people both to become engaged in nonviolent actions and to commit to supporting nonviolent campaigns. There are three popular resistance networks (PRNs) that function as loose organizations to support popular resistance in Area C: Stop the Wall, which was established in 2002 and focuses on advocating and networking with the international community and increasing awareness among Palestinians about their national struggle; the National Committee, which was established in 2004 to support committees with legal struggle and mobilize Palestinians to join collective actions (it works under the umbrella of the Fatah liberation movement); and the Popular Struggle Coordination Committee (PSCC).

External actors are any actors outside the OPT who are connected with the campaigns via their work, their projects, or their support (see Table 5).

Table 5. Domestic and External Actors

TYPES OF ACTORS		
DOMESTIC ACTORS		**EXTERNAL ACTORS**
• Community residents in the OPT • Community organizations in the OPT, including Popular Resistance Committees (PRCs) and Popular Resistance Networks (PRNs) • The project committees and local councils • Palestinian Authority	Campaign members—whether community residents or members of community organizations who are directly involved in campaign actions	Any actors outside of the OPT who are connected with the campaigns

Interconnected Actors and Resources

All resources, whether material or non-material, can be further assessed based on whether they already existed or were produced by the campaign actors themselves, whether from external or domestic actors. Externally accessed and acquired resources are any material or non-material resources that are acquired from external actors or with their help (see Table 6).

Table 6. Actors and Acquisition of Resources

	MATERIAL RESOURCES	NON-MATERIAL RESOURCES
Domestic Actors: Internally Harnessed and/or Harnessed with Grassroots Help	All kinds of material resources provided by domestic actors (internal or community-derived material resources)	All kinds of skills, experience, and knowledge provided by domestic actors (internal, or community-derived, non-material resources)
External Actors: Externally Acquired or Acquired with External Help	All kinds of material resources provided by external actors (externally provided material resources)	All kinds of skills, networks, workshops, training, advocacy, and solidarity developed by domestic actors with external actors' help (non-material resources garnered with external help)

Material and Non-material Resources in the Case Studies

This study found that a wide range of material and non-material resources were secured by the analyzed campaigns. Furthermore, different types of material and non-material resources were each found to have their own particular effects on the nature and outcomes of specific campaign actions. This allowed the identification of important relationships between the nature of resources and campaign capabilities and choices. Tables 7 and 8, on the next page, provide examples of material and non-material resources from the campaigns and assess their nature and impact, as well as the types of actors and resources they provide. Table 7 illustrates examples of material resources from the campaigns in Palestine, while Table 8 illustrates examples of non-material resources. The findings these tables summarize are set out in full detail in the empirical section of the monograph (Chapters 4, 5, and 6), and they help frame the discussion of the role of domestic and external actors which is introduced and elaborated further in the latter part of this study.

Table 7. Examples of Material Resources, Their Nature, Impact, and Actors Derived from Case Studies

EXAMPLE OF MATERIAL RESOURCE	NATURE OF MATERIAL RESOURCE	TYPE OF ACTOR– PROVIDER/ CONTRIBUTOR	IMPACT OF RESOURCE
FINANCIAL RESOURCES			
Monetary donations and grants	Fungible, can be easily converted into other resources needed for the campaign	Domestic and External	Enable activists to buy different kinds of material resources
Income from selling food, T-shirts, and embroideries	Available and affordable	Domestic	Create economic independence and job opportunities
IN-KIND CONTRIBUTIONS			
Canned food	Last longer than perishable food, easy to prepare	Domestic	Enable activists to stay without leaving the place to search for food
Transportation means (cars, buses)	Available and provide help in transporting activists	Domestic and External	Increase number of participants in the campaigns' actions
Donkeys	Available, can transport materials in areas where there are no roads Do not attract attention of the Israeli army and settlers because residents use donkeys daily	Domestic	Secure material resources at the spot where building is taking place
Medical aid kits	Available and portable	External	Help injured activists recover
HUMAN AND ORGANIZATIONAL			
Volunteer labor	Available, easy to secure as a result of the social capital of the community through family relations	Domestic	Make infrastructure activities faster
Skills in making hay-and-clay bricks	Available, part of the tradition of the JV residents	Domestic	Save financial resources and protect the bricks from confiscation by the Israeli army
Skills in solar panel installation	Available through skilled engineers, can be produced by locals who gain key skills	Domestic and External	Make installation faster, create sustainability
Skills in building brick houses	Available, each family has members who have this skill	Domestic	Make building houses faster
Skills in infrastructure projects	Many residents have these skill	Domestic	Make infrastructure activities faster
Local organizational networks	Loose grassroots networks Networks that link the PRCs and the PRNs with NGOs, INGOs etc.	Domestic	Help campaigns harness material and non-material resources
Transnational networks with established international NGOs	Autonomy of action relative to their local counterparts and independent from the Israeli authorities	External	Help campaigns harness material and non-material resources Provide international nonviolent accompaniment embedded within the community that mitigated Israeli oppression Help campaigns have better outreach
BUILDING MATERIALS AND EQUIPMENT			
Building materials (Bricks, cement, gravel, fuel, iron, sand)	Available, easy to transport and hide, and can be used for quick construction and building	Domestic and External	Provide residents with homes to live in Encourage people to stay in their communities
Tractors	Available, can reach off-road areas	Domestic	Secure building materials at the spot where building is taking place

Table 7, cont'd

EXAMPLE OF MATERIAL RESOURCE	NATURE OF MATERIAL RESOURCE	TYPE OF ACTOR– PROVIDER/ CONTRIBUTOR	IMPACT OF RESOURCE
Solar panels	Do not need infrastructure, easy to hide and move in case the Israeli army discovers them	External	Provide residents with electricity that facilitates the life of the residents
Plastic water pipe networks	Light and easy to carry, install, and hide	External	Provide the communities with water
Hay-and-clay bricks	Available, cheap, and can be produced on construction sites	Domestic	Provide residents with homes to live in
Tents	Fast and easy to set-up, easy to transport	External	Protect people from sun and cold weather and encourage people to stay in their communities
Small cameras and laptops	Portable	Domestic and External	Allow the documenting of actions and the writing of reports
Mattresses and sleeping bags, winter covers	Light and easy to carry	External	Help activists stay warm and thus stay longer in the built villages

Table 8. Examples of Non-material Resources, Their Nature, Impact, and Actors Derived from Case Studies

EXAMPLE OF NON-MATERIAL RESOURCE	NATURE OF NON-MATERIAL RESOURCE	TYPE OF ACTOR– PROVIDER/ CONTRIBUTOR	IMPACT OF RESOURCE
CULTURAL RESOURCES			
Life experience in organizing and leading nonviolent actions	Self-produced among activists	Domestic	Spreads nonviolent campaigns, provides protection for activists, increases nonviolent discipline
Technical Knowledge	Gained from external actors	Both	Sustainability of the constructed houses, caves, water networks and renewable energy systems
Legal knowledge	Gained from external actors	Both	Protect material resources and constructed houses
Knowledge of local human and geographic landscape; familiarity with existing grievances and infrastructure needs in the community	Learned from experience and living in the communities	Domestic	Makes transporting material resources safer Helps in choosing sites that the army cannot discover
Experience of the hardship of semi-Bedouin life	Strong sense of belonging to the land and to families Rooted in voluntarism, generosity, nature of work as shepherds and farmers, resilience in the face of hardship	Domestic	Makes volunteer labor available Secures in-kind contributions Makes monitoring soldiers and settlers easier
Committed to traditions such as Onah and Ma'dood	Social tradition set on a mutual aid	Domestic	Increase mutual help and solidarity among residents Increase local participation and availability of voluntary labor
Sumud as the ability to stand steadfast on the land	A philosophy that understands life in multi-generational terms and survival as an unending and ever-present act of resistance to oppression Deeply rooted in the communities	Domestic	Keeps a spirit of defiance toward an occupier alive and promotes inner peace, self-confidence, and love for others

19

EXAMPLE OF NON-MATERIAL RESOURCE	NATURE OF NON-MATERIAL RESOURCE	TYPE OF ACTOR— PROVIDER/ CONTRIBUTOR	IMPACT OF RESOURCE
SOCIAL RESOURCES			
Strong family relations	Deeply personal	Domestic	Help organize nonviolent actions
Strong neighborhood acquaintances	A conduit for communication among residents and knowledge sharing Respect and care for a neighbor	Domestic	Make gathering material resources easier
Strong communal trust among residents	Openness to helping each other and a feeling that one can rely on others in times of need	Domestic	Help recruit material resources for campaigns' actions
Social networks	Intangible and loose groupings based on professional, neighborhood, and social relations	Domestic	Help recruit volunteers

The nature of material and non-material resources has a great impact on the campaigns in which they are mobilized. Tables 7 and 8 also show how the nature of each resource type helps generate other kinds of material and non-material resources. For example, money donated from l'Association France Palestine Solidarité (AFPS) enabled activists in the JVS campaign to buy a school bus. In particular, Table 8 illustrates how the non-material resources of domestic actors were harnessed to acquire material resources. For example, *Onah* enabled activists in the SHH campaign to recruit labor from volunteers who helped construct homes.

Monograph Structure

Building on this study's analytical framework, Chapter 2 explores local responses to the challenges faced by Palestinian residents in Area C through the lens of three case studies. With the help of grassroots activists, the residents of the Palestinian communities in Area C have coordinated and participated in several popular nonviolent campaigns against the Israeli occupation. The case studies take an in-depth look into these campaigns and then consider them through the monograph's analytical framework. Chapter 3 considers the processes and mechanisms that the campaigns used to determine which resources were necessary to carry out campaign actions. Chapter 4 analyzes how the campaigns generated material and non-material resources, whether by harnessing resources already existing in their communities or by acquiring resources from external actors. Chapter 5 reviews the actors involved in the campaigns—both domestic and the external actors that comprise the major outside players in these campaigns. Chapter 6 considers how campaign actors leverage short-term and long-term opportunities for harnessing and acquiring resources. Chapter 7 assesses how campaigns manage the material and non-material resources they have acquired and considers the impact of the campaigns' organizational structures on resource management. Chapter 8 reports how the campaigns conceal material resources from the occupation forces, and Chapter 9 analyzes the impacts of material and non-material resources on the effectiveness of the campaigns. Finally, the Conclusion provides takeaway lessons for practitioners, activists, and external actors, as well as scholars and researchers.

Key Findings of the Monograph

The Palestinian communities living in Area C experience a lack of democracy and economic prosperity due to the Israeli occupation. To add insult to injury, they are also plagued by the internal political divisions that have existed among the various Palestinian liberation movements over decades. Such challenges affect the ability of local activists to source, manage, and deploy resources. While their campaigns have generally lacked a strong communication infrastructure and the skills needed to generate greater material support, this study finds that Palestinian activists have nonetheless managed to secure and use specific material resources to achieve their campaign goals.

The following sections highlight the key findings unearthed throughout this monograph.

Community residents played key roles in the acquisition of material resources for campaigns
The domestic actors in the three campaigns were comprised of the residents of the communities, grassroots PRNs and PRCs, the PNA and some of its ministries (including the ministries of local government, agriculture, and education), and Palestinian NGOs. The residents of the communities were the key domestic actors for the campaigns and provided in-kind contributions, financial donations, and building materials and equipment. They were actively involved in the campaigns' actions and volunteered their time and skills. They were the ones who committed themselves and their families to the campaigns' actions—including the women, who were the cornerstone of efforts to generate financial support thanks to their selling homemade products. Moreover, women played an essential role in protecting building materials.

The residents of the communities relied mainly on themselves to generate material and non-material resources, which enabled them to sustain their campaigns for more than ten years. Their great commitment attracted other external and domestic actors. For example, the PNA provided local campaigns with some monetary and non-monetary resources. It also supported legal defense work by providing lawyers and covering court fees to support activists who had been charged by the Israeli occupation forces. The main material resources offered by the PNA were used for the construction of infrastructure. The Palestinian NGOs provided campaigns—particularly the SHH and JVS campaigns—with infrastructure materials such as solar panels and plastic water pipelines. Meanwhile, the PRNs and PRCs were the main actors who helped acquire material and non-material resources from different domestic and external actors.

Material resources sustained the campaigns and furthered their goals

The analysis of the campaigns demonstrates that community-generated material resources—some derived through non-material resources—were the most valuable to these nonviolent resistance campaigns. The interviewees for this study emphasized that materials generated from domestic rather than external sources have had the greatest impact on nonviolent campaigns in the SHH and the JV. Material resources acquired from external actors were sometimes problematic as the process of their acquisition and management risked producing internal division among activists. Externally acquired material resources were deployed effectively when their type, management, and use were defined and determined by, or in direct consultation with, the affected communities. This decision-making process enhanced community solidarity and the spread of nonviolent resistance. Material resources, and particularly building and infrastructure materials, were the most important resources that enabled campaign actors to build and rebuild houses, renovate water wells and caves, and speed up the construction of infrastructure. These materials played a crucial role in sustaining the campaigns and advancing their objectives, and in the long-term they helped the residents of the JV and the SHH stay resilient in their communities.

Non-material resources were crucial in generating material resources and strengthening campaign actions

Non-material resources helped campaigns generate material resources, including financial resources, in-kind contributions, and human and organizational resources. Such resources were used by campaigns to build houses and new infrastructure. Also, non-material resources such as community networks and family relationships have enabled communities to mobilize more residents, organize coordinated actions, and promote their campaigns. Because of the skillful acquisition and use of non-material resources, the SHH campaign has branched out across local communities, such as the Re-exist campaign in Al Mufaqara, the Susya community's campaign, and the Youth of Sumud campaign in the Sarura community dedicated to returning forcibly displaced people to their lands. Similarly, the RV campaign spread to different sites in the OPT when they managed to build eight villages. The JVS campaign also managed to encompass many communities in the JV, from the north to the south. Furthermore, non-material resources such as the semi-Bedouin lifestyle of the residents and their in-depth knowledge of the area helped protect material resources from confiscation by the Israeli authorities.

Campaign strategies and processes played a strategic role both in the acquisition of material resources and in harnessing non-material resources for campaign purposes

After analyzing the three campaigns launched to resist the forced displacement of Palestinians, this monograph concludes that the organizers of the campaigns adopted different strategies that are crucial both in the acquisition of material resources and in harnessing non-material resources available at the grassroots level. First, campaign members relied on family relations and family members to promote the campaigns, share information about them, and recruit volunteers. Campaign actors benefited from the semi-Bedouin lifestyle of the JV and SHH communities, as well as from the rich networks that linked the PRNs with domestic and outside actors and helped them to acquire material and non-material resources. Expert activists shared their experiences with locals and relied on cohesive relations between PRCs and local councils, and the activists' dual roles and responsibilities as members of the PRCs and the local councils helped them to harness material resources from the residents.

Second, the campaigns' members tapped into the communities' urgent needs and demands to generate material resources. The communities targeted in the three campaigns lacked basic services such as housing, electricity, water, and roads. Third, despite the fact that the campaigns were community-based and aimed to solve the problems of those communities, activists managed to link them with the Palestinian national struggle to end the occupation, which helped generate material resources from the PNA and the political parties. Fourth, activists utilized the opportunity for action created by dramatic events and common threats, as well as triumphs in legal struggles, to generate material resources in the SHH, JVS, and the RV campaigns. Fifth, the campaign actors' first-hand experience of hardship and living the communal lifestyle helped harness material and non-material resources from the communities themselves. This laid the groundwork for activists to organize visits to the sites with professional consultants, confer with residents, and hold meetings with domestic and international actors interested in outreach and networking with external actors to provide the campaigns with needed materials. This process helped the organizers determine what kinds of material resources they needed and how to acquire them, based on local expertise.

This monograph also concludes that face-to-face meetings between campaign members and local residents enabled them to generate material resources. The organizers could overcome limited access to material resources under foreign occupation by prioritizing the effective use of existing non-material resources in semi-Bedouin communities, including relationships between families, strong connections with neighbors, and social networks between people in and across cities and towns. In other words, they utilized customs and traditions to mobilize residents. The organizers also harnessed cultural capital built on history, collective memory, and the spirit of everyday resistance represented by *Sumud* and *Onah*. These non-material resources are rooted in the social capital of Palestinian communities. Another significant mechanism used to generate material resources was ensuring media coverage. Finally, activists organized tours for representatives of the PNA, NGOs, and INGOs, which served as a good strategy for generating material resources from these actors.

External actors played supportive roles for the key domestic campaign drivers
This study concludes that external actors came from a wide range of organizations, from solidarity groups to aid organizations and INGOs because of grassroots activists planning and launching the campaigns. External actors supported the three campaigns with material resources needed for their actions. They also played a role in enabling the campaign actors to network with other international organizations. The external actors' role was particularly important to the campaigns through offering capacity-building training and helping grassroots activists generate financial contributions and grants directly and indirectly. They enabled the campaigns to reach their respective home countries, and this, in turn, helped the campaigns to generate material resources. This study showed that external solidarity groups such as International Solidarity Movement (ISM) and others played the largest supporting role among external actors.

The availability of material resources affected the campaign outcomes
The three campaigns achieved different outcomes as a result movement actors' ability to secure, use, and manage material and non-material resources. This research found that the availability of material resources sped up the rebuilding of many of the demolished houses and increased the construction of new houses in the three campaigns. One of the significant outcomes of the SHH and JVS campaigns resulting from the availability of material resources were that water networks reached every single home in these communities. Water networks were also maintained, and renewable energy was made available. In the RV campaign, activists managed to delay the annexation of the areas by Israel, and this encouraged Bedouins to live in those places. In other areas, this strategy encouraged farmers to reach their land and cultivate it. Material resources were the fuel that helped residents continue their lives in the SHH and JV communities.

Effective management of resources helped maintain campaigns' effectiveness and unity
The research proves that effective management of resources enabled activists to achieve the goals of the campaigns with the resources they acquired. Activists in the three campaigns adopted various strategies to manage material resources effectively. Their first strategy was to use the minimum quantity of material resources to maximize campaign goals. This required establishing an effective organizational structure that included a clear set of priorities and agreement on the clear division of tasks and responsibilities so that the operation could function well. To effectively manage material and non-material resources, the organizers employed joint planning with residents, mapping of residents' available skills and knowledge, and working as a team in the campaigns. In managing material resources, activists relied on cohesive relationships between project committees, local councils, the PRCs, the PRNs (via the PSCC), and donors.

Interviewees explained that management issues were also impacted by the kinds of resources that needed to be managed at any given time. Mixed management between domestic and external donors helped, on the one hand, to ensure that there were enough of the right kinds of materials. On the other hand, this enabled the realization of effective local management of materials. Working closely allowed people to build trust between locals and donors.

The management of material resources garnered from the residents was organized in harmony with cultural norms and traditions, which contributed to maintaining campaign momentum despite the lack of organizational networks such as local councils and NGOs. Coordination and the inclusion of the PRNs in managing material and non-material resources fostered unity and maintenance of the campaigns.

This study also asserts that the different characters of campaigns—whether long-term or short-term—impacted the demand for resources. Long-term campaigns need more resources and time to garner necessary material and non-material resources than their shorter-term counterparts. The management and allocation of material resources in long-term campaigns in a context of repression and internal division also requires long-term vision and appropriate strategies. For example, organizers need to be able to manage motivation and its potential decline over time as well as to cater for emergencies, such as the arrest and jailing of key personnel.

Ultimately, the ability to use and manage material and non-material resources effectively has increased both the number of residents involved in nonviolent campaigns and the effectiveness of these campaigns.

Chapter 2. The Political and Territorial Background of the Campaigns

This chapter describes the background and actions of the three campaigns. For context, it first defines Area C in relation to the different Israeli categorizations and divisions of the West Bank. This enables the reader to understand the long-term Israeli strategy and objective to forcibly displace Palestinian communities from Area C. After providing the political, historical, and geographic backgrounds, this chapter tells the stories of the campaigns organized by community residents living in Area C. For each of the three campaigns, it first describes their locations. It then explains the challenges the Palestinian residents face under the Israeli occupation, from forced displacement to the lack of basic rights in education, health, and housing. Finally, it analyzes the tactics adopted by grassroots activists to counter the Israeli violations of their rights and it highlights the similarities and differences between each of the three campaigns.

This study finds that the Israeli occupation authorities designed their policies to forcibly displace Palestinians in order to annex the land but not the people. It also finds that the campaigns in the South Hebron Hills (SHH) and the Jordan Valley (JV) aimed to protect the people and their right to remain on their land. On the other hand, the Rebuilding Villages (RV) campaign aimed to preserve the land from Israeli annexation. The chapter also finds that, in the JV and the SHH, the campaigns were initially started by local community residents but eventually succeeded in mobilizing more Palestinian and international supporters to join their actions. The RV campaign was organized by PRNs that relied on existing networks and relationships. This campaign was proactive in the sense that the organizers generated resources before the campaign actions took place. The SHH and JVS campaigns arose in response to the daily violations of the residents' rights and were thus reactive. The campaign actors gradually accumulated resources during the implementation of the campaigns. They first began by harnessing community-based material and non-material resources and then they sought resources externally.

Despite the similar problems faced by the SHH and JVS campaigns, activists adopted tactics that specifically suited their campaign goals. This chapter finds that the nonviolent tactics used in the three campaigns relied on specific material and non-material resources that activists managed to mobilize locally.

Area C Context

For more than five decades, Palestinians in the OPT have been living under an Israeli military occupation that has dispersed their communities and prevented them from exercising their basic human rights. Although the United Nations recognizes the West Bank, East Jerusalem, and the Gaza Strip as occupied territories without legal or political distinctions between their types of occupation, the map of the West Bank (Figure 3 on page 29) shows clearly how the Oslo II agreement, signed in 1995, divided the occupied West Bank into three distinct categories:

- **Area A** constitutes 18 percent of the area of the West Bank and under the terms of the agreement should now be under full Palestinian control.

- **Area B** represents 21 percent of the West Bank, with the PNA responsible for civil affairs and the Israeli government responsible for land and security.

- **Area C** covers 61 percent of the West Bank and is fully under Israeli control.

The status of Area C was left as a matter with outstanding issues to be resolved after the 1995 Accords were implemented. The area was to be gradually transferred under Palestinian jurisdiction (Text of Oslo Accords 1993). Despite these terms, illegal Israeli settlements currently occupy 17 percent of Area C, where the Israeli authorities have kept building settlements and the number of settlers has tripled since the Oslo agreement. 441,600 Israeli settlers live in Area C (Peace Now 2019), in addition to the 209,270 settlers living in East Jerusalem (B'Tselem 2019). A further 30 percent of the area is zoned by the Israeli occupation as closed and designated for military training. When all restrictions are factored in, a full 70 percent of Area C comprises land that Palestinians are prohibited to build on, 29 percent is inhabited by 300,000 Palestinians who are living there without Israeli permission, and only in the remaining 1 percent are building permissions granted. Most Palestinians living in Area C are farmers and Bedouins and rely on their land and livestock. There are 27,500 Bedouin Palestinians living in places from which Israel can evict them at any time.[6] In fact, the Israeli forces have been displacing them and other Palestinians since the Nakba in 1948.[7]

In contravention of the Oslo Accords' stated aims, the Israeli government has increased its activities in Area C and placed more restrictions on Palestinians living there (Peace Now

---

6   Bedouins live in Area C, particularly in areas close to the borders (such as the Jordan Valley and the SHH) and in areas considered by the Israeli authorities as firing zones or closed military zones. The residents of these areas are the most vulnerable because they are being forcibly displaced and threatened by Israeli forces to a greater extent than other residents of Area C.

7   *Nakba* is the Arabic word for "catastrophe" and describes what happened to the Palestinians when, in the 1948 war, Israel expelled more than 700,000 Palestinians who became refugees in the West Bank, Gaza, and neighboring Arab countries.

2018). The latest Israeli plan, as of April 2020, is to annex 50 percent of Area C, a move which contravenes the Oslo Accords and violates international law. In addition to building settlements and closed military zones, Israel has closed other parts of Area C as natural resources and confiscated land for bypass roads. This has further narrowed Palestinian lands and has negatively affected their life. Moreover, Israel has continued withholding building permits, refuses to recognize Palestinian villages and hamlets, and continues to demolish their houses.

Israeli Strategy and Objectives in Area C

Israel's strategy of oppression in Area C and the different restrictions on Palestinian residents is aimed at making their lives impossible so that they will move from Area C to Areas A and B under the Palestinian Authority. On the one hand, Israel restricts Palestinians from staying on their land through house demolitions, severe restrictions on planned building projects, and by limiting access to natural resources. On the other hand, the Israeli authorities continue to confiscate Palestinian land and build settlements. They have also been oppressing Palestinians through arrests and systematic violence against them.

The long-term objective is to force the Palestinian residents to resettle into Area A and B without their land so that Israel can annex Area C, build more and extend existing settlements, and establish full control over Area C's resources. Politically, the Israeli authorities' actions have already created a de facto annexation of Area C that will influence the creation of a Palestinian state. Israel's policy in Area C is rooted in a perception of the area as meant, above all, to serve Israeli needs at the expense of Palestinians'. As such, Israel consistently takes actions that strengthen its hold on Area C, displace the Palestinian presence, exploit the area's resources, and serve to bring about a permanent situation in which Israeli settlements thrive and the Palestinian presence is negligible (B'Tselem 2013).

The international community has failed to effectively pressure the Israeli government, as an occupying power, to respect the rights of the Palestinians living in Area C. Moreover, the bias of successive United States administrations in favor of Israel has encouraged the Israeli government to continue building illegal settlements, confiscating Palestinian land, and ethnically cleansing Palestinians from region. Under the terms of the Trump administration's plan, released in January 2020, only 40 percent of Area C would be transferred back to the Palestinians (White House 2020). This parallels the Israeli government's intentions to annex the majority, if not the whole, of Area C. The Israeli government officially announced that it will start the annexation of parts of Area C by the beginning of July 2020. While the official annexation was postponed as a result of the normalization of relations between some Arab regimes and Israel, settlers still attempt to grab more land, and Israeli violations have continued.

United Nations Office for the Coordination of Humanitarian Affairs
occupied Palestinian territory
West Bank: Area C Map

February 2011

Border

--- International Border

--- Green Line

▨ Israeli Unilaterally Declared Municipal Area of Jerusalem[1]

1. In 1967, Israel occupied the West Bank and unilaterally annexed to its territory 70.5 km of the occupied area

Barrier

—— Constructed / Under Construction

—-—- Planned

Oslo Agreement[2]

▨ Area (A), (B)

▨ Area C & Nature Reserves

Oslo Interim Agreement

2. Area A : Full Palestinian civil and security control
Area B: Full Palestinian civil control and joint Israeli-Palestinian security control
Area C: Full Israeli control over security, planning and construction

United Nations Office for the Coordination of Humanitarian Affairs
Cartography: OCHA-oPt - February 2011. Base data: OCHA, PA MoP, JRC update 08. For comments contact <ochaopt@un.org> or Tel. +972 (02) 582-9962 http://www.ochaopt.org

FIGURE 3. Occupied West Bank Areas A, B, and C

Source: OCHA-oPt 2011

The Palestinian National Authority (PNA) and Palestinian political parties—such as Fatah and some of the left-wing parties which maintain formal contacts and political, economic, and security agreements with the Israeli government—failed to exercise effective pressure on the occupier and, in essence, neglected Palestinians' basic needs and further undermined the resilience of local communities (Soliman 2019, Darweish and Rigby 2015). For example, the PNA failed to implement the budget allocated to help Area C communities develop specific housing and infrastructure projects or to make use of the natural resources of Area C such as water and land (Shbaita 2018).[8]

The Palestinians in Area C have independently organized and launched a variety of nonviolent campaigns to protect their right to remain and live in Area C and to defend their land, families, and property. This study assesses three grassroots resistance campaigns in Area C of the West Bank that adopted a variety of nonviolent resistance methods, ranging from disruptive, direct collective actions such as sit-ins, demonstrations, marches, and nonviolent interventions to acts of constructive resistance such as building and rebuilding houses, creating basic village infrastructure, and cultivating land. The campaigns were specifically selected to demonstrate how local activists secured, managed, and deployed material and non-material resources in support of their campaigns and to show how these resources have affected the fortunes of these campaigns. While this research has been based on specific campaigns, the monograph offers an analytical model and in-depth case study analysis that others can emulate to identify and assess both how different kinds of resources are acquired and integrated into campaign activities and what impact they have on a campaign's success.

The study focuses on the following campaigns:

1. The campaign in the South Hebron Hills (SHH).

2. The Jordan Valley Solidarity (JVS) campaign, also called "We Exist to Resist."

3. The campaign to Rebuild Villages (RV) in Area C and other locations in East Jerusalem and south of Jericho.

Table 9 summarizes the three campaigns in terms of their locations, aims, challenges, and the problems they faced, as well as the nonviolent actions deployed by the campaigns.

---

8   In the government plan for the years 2017–2022, the PNA allocated budget to support Area C communities, but these plans have not been implemented, and the PNA's involvement in Area C has remained reactive and has not matched the peoples' needs (Shbaita 2018).

Table 9. Summary of the Three Nonviolent Campaigns

CAMPAIGN	GEOGRAPHICAL LOCATION	PROBLEMS AND CHALLENGES	AIM OF THE CAMPAIGN	ACTIONS
South Hebron Hills campaign, 1999–Present	Southern region of the West Bank	• Forced eviction • Prevented from building houses • No access to electricity and water	To protect the rights of the residents of the SHH by: • Resisting house demolitions • Resisting settlement expansions • Resisting the building of the separation wall	• Rehabilitate caves and water wells • Build tents and brick houses for farmers • Rebuild structures destroyed by the Israeli army • Build roads so people can easily access their homes • Organize collective direct actions • Rehabilitate and cultivate the land and plant trees • Accompany children on their way to school • Develop infrastructure, including solar panels, water pipelines, and water wells • Organize annual popular resistance festivals • Access the land in the face of settler attacks • Reoccupy the forcibly evicted villages and encourage new residents to come and live in these areas
Jordan Valley Solidarity campaign ("We Exist to Resist"), 2003–Present	The JV in the northeast region of the West Bank	• Forced eviction through house demolitions • Arbitrary arrest and detention • Land confiscations • Movement restriction and curfews • Denial of access to water, electricity, health, and education	To protect Palestinian existence in the JV	• Build community schools • Help several communities run water pipes to their local area • Mobilize local communities around rebuilding structures destroyed by the Israeli occupation • Build roads so people can easily access their homes • Mobilize and educate JV communities about the traditional methods of building with homemade hay-and-clay bricks • Plant trees to preserve the land
Rebuilding Villages campaign, 2013–2015	Various sites around East Jerusalem and south of Jericho	• No access to the land • Threat of annexation	To protect the land from annexation by the Israeli government	• Build villages • Organize various direct nonviolent actions • Help Palestinians move to and live in the villages

The South Hebron Hills (SHH) Campaign: 1999–Present

Geographic location	South Hebron Hills
Campaign period	1999 to the present
Territorial scope	30 villages and hamlets
Beneficiaries	Residents of the South Hebron Hills
Amount of mobilized people	Thousands of participants
Number of campaign events	More than 400 nonviolent actions
Scope of study	1999–2018

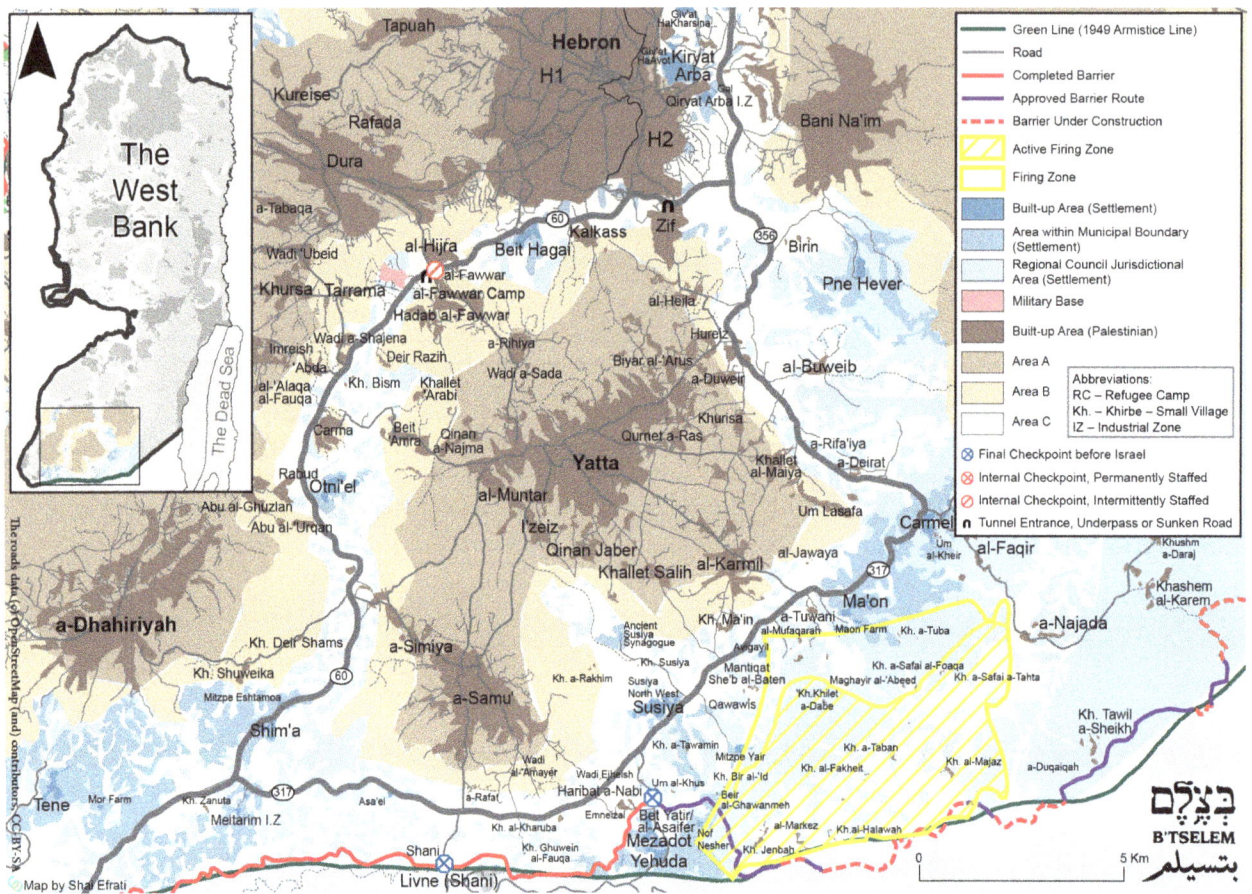

FIGURE 4. South Hebron Hills Area

Source: B'Tselem

Location of the SHH Campaign

The SHH area, known in Arabic as *Masafer Yatta*, is located 26 kilometers to the south of Hebron (see Figure 4). It is located within Area C of the OPT, which was placed under full Israeli control after the Oslo Accords were signed by the Palestinian Liberation Organization (PLO) and the Israeli government in September 1993. The SHH consists of 28 Palestinian hamlets, including Al Tuwani village, which is the geographic center of Masafer Yatta. The area inhabited by 15 communities in the SHH is recognized by the Israeli occupation as a firing zone, which means that the Israeli army can evict residents during military training and forbid Palestinians from constructing anything in this area. The area inhabited by the remainder of the communities is recognized as Area C. Al Tuwani is the only community recognized by the Israeli authorities where Palestinians can build in areas specifically designated in the master plan. The area is no larger than 33 dunums, or 3.3 hectares—equivalent to approximately four soccer fields—and it is still classified as part of Area C. According to the Palestinian Central Bureau of Statistics (2017), the area has a population of 3,000 Palestinians. Yet the communities are distributed across the hills of South Hebron on about 250,000 dunums, or 25,000 hectares, of land. The population of each community ranges from 20 to 500 residents. The communities' main sources of income are farming and shepherding, and their people live a semi-nomadic life (Isaac 2009). The constant Israeli military presence in the SHH made the securing and redistribution of material resources for campaign purposes a challenge to the organizers. At the same time, the geography of the SHH, where small hamlets are scattered across the hills, helped activists hide and protect material resources such as building materials.

Hardship and Repression of the SHH Residents

According to United Nations reports (OCHA-oPt 2013) and human rights organizations (B'Tselem 2017), the SHH villagers face forced eviction while being prevented from building houses and accessing basic services such as electricity and water. The Israeli government has worked to make life difficult for residents. The aim has been to displace them from the SHH, replace these communities with Israeli settlements, and connect the settlements with each other to form a chain that will reach larger Israeli towns in the south.

SHH residents suffer direct violence from the Israeli settlers and army. Israeli attacks are not limited to people but are also directed against their livestock and land. Furthermore, the Israeli army prevents residents from cultivating their land and isolates and divides the communities by building walls and settlements.

The Israeli government has taken several measures to make it impossible for the residents to remain on their land. For example, it has repeatedly blocked the entrances to the villages and established checkpoints to disconnect the SHH from other towns. The Israeli occupation forces have also built a wall parallel to Road 317 which cuts off the people south of the road from the big Palestinian town of Yatta and other towns and villages to its north (see Figure 4), impeding their movement with the eventual goal of forcing them to leave.

During the 1970s, around 38,000 dunums (close to 9,400 acres) of land in the SHH were designated as a firing zone by the Israeli government. One activist explains, "The Israeli army was doing military exercises at specific times during the summer when the agricultural crops are dry; when they start shooting, they burn the crops to maximize the loss of the farmers."[9]

These restrictions and the encroachment into SHH by the Israeli occupation authorities were achieved through gradual repression over time so as to minimize Palestinian resistance and obscure the SHH residents' understanding of Israeli policies and intentions. The mayor of one hamlet confirmed that the residents did not resist the building of Road 317 because initially the road was being used more by Palestinians than by settlers. Only later did it become clear that it had been constructed to incentivize settlers to build new settlements.

The PRC comprises grassroots activists from various communities who are responsible for organizing popular nonviolent resistance.

Israeli policies escalated in 1999 when their forces started demolishing houses and the ancient water wells that were the only source of water for SHH residents. They also continued to refuse permits to build houses, schools, water pipelines, and power grids. In other words, Israeli policies prevented the communities from maintaining their infrastructure. The Israeli civil administration refused to give civic entities master plans and the kinds of formal recognition that would have given them rights and access to infrastructure. Similarly, the Israeli army destroyed power grids and alternative energy sources that residents had established in their communities. The people in the SHH also faced direct violence from settlers and the army in the form of physical attacks, such as burning their tents, chopping down their olive trees, and poisoning water wells and pastures. All these Israeli policies cultivated a fear among the people that crippled any organizing of collective actions.

However, these events helped mobilize material resources from domestic and external sources. When, in November 1999, 15 communities were expelled from their land, local people were galvanized against the Israeli occupation. They began holding meetings and discussions about the strategies and tactics that would help secure their rights to housing, education, and the use of their own land. People looked for strategies to prevent further evictions. The coordinator of the SHH campaign explains that "after November 1999, we thought about our tactics in light of this dramatic event. Therefore, we held a series of meetings with the people of the SHH and decided to launch the SHH nonviolent campaign."[10] They established a PRC soon afterward and launched a campaign against forced displacement that continues to this day.

---

9 Interview with the head of one of the hamlets in the SHH, 5 May 2019.

10 Interview with the coordinator of the SHH campaign, south of the West Bank, 1 May 2019.

The PRC comprises grassroots activists from various SHH communities who are committed to and responsible for organizing popular nonviolent resistance in the area. The aim of the PRC was to mobilize residents and persuade them to join collective actions. It was tasked with garnering material and non-material resources for the campaign and coordinating with local project committees and councils, in addition to the heads of local families.[11]

The central SHH campaign consisted of different small campaigns in some of the communities: these included the Re-exist campaign in Al Mufaqara that managed to build 15 brick houses for the community's residents (between 2011 and 2013); the Susya campaign that prevented the villagers from being evicted (2006 to the present); and the Um al Khaier campaign that prevented the demolition of community houses and rebuilt homes (from 2006 to the present). Furthermore, the Youth of Sumud campaign in SHH, which began in 2017, is rehabilitating caves for the Sarura community in a bid to bring back families that were evicted by Israeli forces in 1999.

The SHH Campaign Actions

When everything is forbidden, then everything you do is resistance; whenever there is occupation, your role is to resist.[12]

From 1999 onward, SHH residents adopted various civil resistance tactics and leveraged institutional mechanisms in the form of legal actions. They rehabilitated caves and water wells, built tents and brick houses, rebuilt structures destroyed by the Israeli army, built roads, organized collective direct actions, developed infrastructure (including solar panels and water pipelines), organized annual popular resistance festivals, and reoccupied the forcibly evicted villages. The activists also managed to build networks with Israeli activist groups—such as Ta'ayush and Anarchists Against the Wall—and Israeli human rights organizations—such as B'Tselem and Rabbis for Human Rights (these and other external actors are described in greater detail in Chapter 5).

They networked with international solidarity groups such as the International Solidarity Movement (ISM), which is a Palestinian-led organization established by Palestinians and international allies in 2002, and international humanitarian and human rights organizations such as Oxfam and Action Aid. This enabled them to secure external material resources, mainly in the form of financial contributions, to cover the legal fees for lawsuits in the Israeli courts that were contesting the eviction of 15 communities. Tents and building materials were

---

11   The project committees are the committees that represent the communities in the Palestinian government. The status of a project committee is lower than that of a local council. The local council is an elected committee that represents the villagers and is responsible for providing public service to them.

12   Interview with the coordinator of the SHH campaign, south of the West Bank, 1 May 2019.

also provided by humanitarian organizations. Meanwhile, the residents of Al Tuwani made in-kind contributions when they shared their homes, food, and water with other evicted residents from the 15 communities and helped them survive and return to their land following the court ruling.

The activists also mobilized domestic non-material resources, including customs and traditions such as *Onah*, which reinforced and motivated generosity and care for neighbors as residents provided food, mattresses, and welcome into their homes for distressed locals. Knowledge, access, and publicity gained from connections with external networks also worked as non-materials resources. Their actions fostered communal solidarity among SHH residents, and it encouraged them to donate monetary and non-monetary materials. It also led them to volunteer their time, skills, and experience to the campaign from its inception. The residents shared their first-hand stories about their oppression at the hands of the Israeli authorities with human right organizations, Israeli and international groups, and Palestinian officials. In early 2000, when the head of Al Mufaqara community was invited to the Israeli parliament to give a speech about the eviction of the communities, it generated sympathy, which, in turn, generated material contributions in the form of tents and financial support.

The campaign organizers developed their campaign tactics based on the needs of the residents. Most of the SHH residents were living in caves and relied on gathered winter water in wells. Thus, they rebuilt structures destroyed by the Israeli army such as brick homes, tents, shelters, and water pipelines, and they developed infrastructure, including solar panels, water wells, and more water pipelines. They were able to build 19 schools, install 40 km of plastic water pipelines, and lay 40 km of roads.

One of the main actions was to rehabilitate caves and water wells. According to the SHH mayor, more than 260 caves and water wells have been rehabilitated from 1999 to 2018. Agricultural land destroyed by the Israeli army was rehabilitated. Infrastructural development projects were started. Residents renovated ancient caves for 50 families and began living in them as a way of "restoring their cultural heritage."[13] They installed 60 solar panels and water pipelines and dug water wells.

Local activists rebuilt demolished houses and constructed new ones. Campaign organizers used the tactic of building tents as a fast way to offer residents places to stay. They also used the tactic of building brick houses to solve housing problems. They have managed to build more than 100 brick homes in different communities in the region. For example, in 2012 they built 15 brick homes in Al Mufaqara.

_____

13   Interview with a youth activist from one of the SHH hamlets, 27 May 2019.

Activists relied on SHH residents who mostly provided them with material resources such as labor and skills, but they also benefited from non-monetary materials that were made available from domestic and external actors through grants and donations in the forms of aid and solidarity. Activists organized annual popular resistance festivals and conferences where hundreds of people attended from different communities throughout the SHH, and effective media coverage of these events mobilized domestic and external actors to provide activists with various resources.[14] In July 2013, the PRCs organized the 6th annual popular resistance conference in Al Mufaqara (Bollack 2013). Activists also reoccupied evicted villages such as Sarura and Al Rakiz and encouraged their relatives in Yatta city to move to these areas. As one activist explained, "the hope was that these new residents would bring life back to the villages."[15]

After 1999, the SHH campaign moved gradually from less visible, individual-led, everyday forms of resistance to include collective actions.

Direct, collective, nonviolent actions such as weekly sit-ins and demonstrations ran alongside these practical initiatives and became the driving force of the nonviolent campaign. After 1999, the SHH campaign moved gradually from less visible, individual-led, everyday forms of resistance such as cultivating land, grazing sheep, and rebuilding homes to include collective actions such as demonstrations, sit-ins, and constructing buildings and infrastructure. This evolution is directly linked with the new resources that became available as the campaign progressed. For example, once they secured the money and the land, they collectively built the school of Al Tuwani.

Despite the risk of retaliation, SHH activists organized collective, nonviolent actions such as weekly sit-ins and demonstrations with dozens and sometimes hundreds of participants. They also organized more than 30 demonstrations to reopen village entrances after the Israeli army blocked them with large stones and soil. The mayor of Al Tuwani explains:

We were going—men, women, and youth united—with simple tools, and we opened the blockade. They continued setting up blockades and we continued bringing them down. They gave up and we didn't give up until we had our village back on the map. I never remember the entrance being closed more than a week, while in other large villages the blockade stayed for months.[16]

_____

14 Popular resistance festivals are events organized by campaign members to celebrate campaign successes and to generate further support for the campaign. For example, when they finished building the school in Al Tuwani, the residents gathered, took part in folk dancing, and gave speeches to the people. Other festivals also took place at the end of the summer camp.

15 Interview with the coordinator of the Sarura campaign, SHH, 7 May 2019.

16 Interview with the Mayor of Al Tuwani, South Hebron Hills, 20 May 2019.

The campaign organizers adopted a tactic of using legal defense mechanisms to support prisoners, prevent house demolishing and defend their land. This happened through qualified lawyers to defend activists in the military courts. For example, the PSCC signed a contract with Gaby Laski's office in Tel Aviv so that its team of Israeli human right lawyers could become partners with the PSCC in defending the activists. The former coordinator of a PRN confirmed:

We chose Israeli lawyers because they speak the same language and they are aware in the Israeli law. Also, they are more able to challenge the court and the military prosecution cannot punish them while the Palestinians cannot do that and easily they can punish them.[17]

Also, campaign organizers conducted cycles of workshops on security issues and protection for activists As the founder of one of the PRNs said:

The legal protection of activists was improved through the establishment of a legal department within the PRCs. The PRNs have been connected to other legal organizations and networks through mechanisms to follow up legal assistance, and more qualified lawyers have been employed for the PRCs. Donors have funded legal defense, international legal campaigns were organized against occupation. We acquired funds for legal fees for arrested activists, against land annexation and house demolishing.[18]

The SHH campaign is centered around resources because the campaign's actors realized their importance for implementing specific actions: to build houses they required labor and building materials; to renovate caves and water wells they needed labor and skills; and to install working infrastructure they required water pipelines and solar panels.

The Jordan Valley Solidarity (JVS) Campaign ("We Exist to Resist"): 2003–Present

Geographic location	**The Jordan Valley**
Campaign period	**2003–Present**
Territorial scope	**27 villages and hamlets**
Beneficiaries	**Residents of the Jordan Valley**
Amount of mobilized people	**Thousands of participants**
Number of campaign events	**More than 200 nonviolent actions**
Scope of study	**2003–2018**

---

17   Interview with the coordinator of the PSCC network, Ramallah, 16 June 2019.

18   Interview with the co-founder of one of the PRNs, center of the West Bank, 7 May 2019.

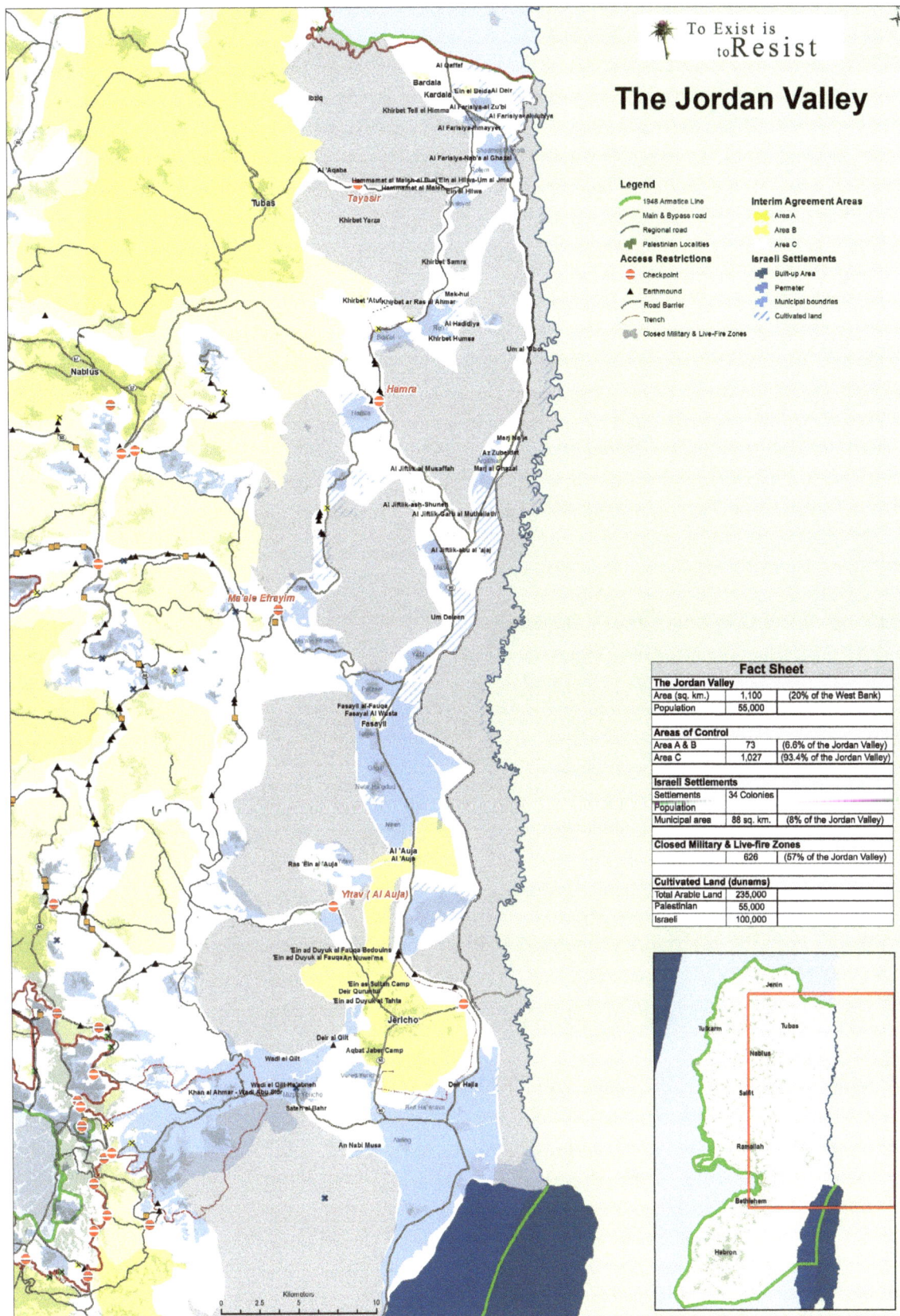

FIGURE 5. Map of the Jordan Valley.

Source: Jordan Valley Solidarity Campaign

Location of the JVS Campaign

The Jordan Valley (JV) covers almost one-third of the West Bank, extending from the Green Line in the north to the Dead Sea in the south, and resting between the hills of the West Bank and the Jordan River to the east. It is home to approximately 6,500 inhabitants who live in 18 semi-nomadic, pastoral communities in the north of the occupied West Bank (see Figure 5). Each village is home to between 50 and 1,000 residents, who all live in tents or shelters without basic services. The JV communities are small, and they are distributed across a huge area surrounded by nine illegal Israeli settlements (with 12,800 settlers), military training zones, and several settlers' farms established across 85 square kilometers. The Israeli government recognizes almost 50 percent of the valley as the state's land. They also declared parts of the JV as closed military zones, firing zones, and nature reserves.

The main sources of income for JV residents are agriculture and shepherding. That the JV is mostly a large plain presents challenges to activists who want to transport material resources discreetly, yet activists are able to make hay-and-clay bricks from its soil, a key resource for building houses.

Hardship and Repression of the JV Residents

Like the SHH, the Jordan Valley is located in Area C. However, the Israeli government has a greater interest in maintaining control over the JV than any other parts of Area C because it has the most fertile land and includes the largest natural water reservoir in the OPT. As a result, the occupation's oppressive acts against JV residents are more constant and frequent than elsewhere. JV communities are living under constant threat of forced displacement. In the early 1990s, the Israeli government built a highway called Road 90 that cut the JV into two parts, leaving residents with very limited access to the eastern part of the valley and inhibiting their movements. (They continued to expand the highway until 2018.)

After signing the Oslo Accords in 1993, the Israeli authorities encouraged Israeli settlers to come and farm in the JV by providing them with land and water, and the Israeli army quickened the pace and extent of its demolitions of JV residents' houses. Most JV communities are under demolition or eviction orders, which is why their very existence should be understood as an act of resistance. A Palestinian farmer living in the north echoed the story of Sisyphus when he recounted that in 2013 the Israeli army had destroyed his sheds and tents 32 times in less than a month: "They were destroying in the morning, and I was rebuilding in the evening. Finally, they got tired, which is why I am still here."[19] He explained the difficulties he faced in transporting material resources to the site on the backs of his donkeys. His natural

---

19   Interview with an activist from the north of the JV, 18 June 2019.

advantage was the fact that his 24 sons and daughters helped him rebuild the tents and the sheds. Tents and volunteers enabled the farmer to stay resilient on his land.

The JV is one of the areas that is declared to be part of Israel in the plan set forward by Trump's administration. Since the signing of the Oslo Accords in 1993, Israel's plans to annex the JV has created fear among the local Palestinian residents and increased mistrust toward the PNA; its support is seen as insufficient, and there is a popular suspicion that the PNA has a tacit agreement with Israel to annex the JV. As a volunteer worker with the JVS campaign explained, "What I fear is the presence of an agreement between the PNA and Israel for the exchange of lands in the JV and to empty these lands of the Palestinian residents. We do not want any material resources from them. Our demand from the PNA is that they do not harm us."[20] The annexation of the JV is a continuous Israeli plan which explains the escalation of Israeli violations of residents' rights. The lack of basic infrastructure in Palestinian communities hinders external communication. Furthermore, it is challenging for activists to travel long distances for face-to-face meetings due to restrictions imposed on their movements. This hardship has a negative impact on their ability to generate material resources and transport them safely.

In its long-term annexation policy for the valuable JV, the Israeli government has relied on an economic strategy to control and co-opt the local people. Since 1967, it has offered Palestinian children and women jobs in the settlers' farms as wage labor, and this has inhibited their participation in the JVS campaign. The Israeli employers usually threaten Palestinian workers with dismissal if they engage in any act or campaign against the Israeli occupation. Since 1948, forced displacement has been pursued through house demolition, movement restrictions, curfews, arbitrary arrests and detentions, land confiscations, and the denial of access to water, electricity, health, and education. This has resulted in a dramatic reduction of the Palestinian population in the area. For example, Al-Mkhoul village to the north of the JV has been demolished more than ten times in the last decade. In 1967, the residents of the JV, including Jericho, east of Nablus countryside, and the southeast Tubas countryside, numbered 320,000, while in 2017 there were just 60,000 residents—a decrease of over 80 percent during a 50-year period (PCBS 2018). According to the 2017 Palestinian Central Bureau Statistics report, 50,000 Palestinians were expelled from the north of the valley. This reduction explains why the remaining residents regard their very existence in the JV as an act of resistance.

Following the 1967 war, Israel's gradual occupation divided the area into different categories, such as military zones, farm settlements, nature reserves, and residential settlements,

---

20   Ibid.

41

which made it much harder for activists to acquire, harness, and redistribute resources to further any of their campaigns.

The Israeli restrictions create major challenges for local volunteers when working in some areas of the JV to secure material resources. Israeli checkpoints at the entrances to the JV constrain domestic and external actors transporting much-needed material resources to the campaign. The coordinator of the JVS noted one incident in 2014 in which "Israelis prevented the representative of the French consulate from entering Al-Mkhoul village. She was attacked and the supplies were confiscated."[21] These checkpoints are also very dangerous to cross. Since 2015, three Palestinians have been killed at Al Hamra checkpoint.

Despite the problems posed by Israeli policies, the lack of communication infrastructure, and skills deficits, the activists in the JV managed to establish PRCs and launch the JVS campaign in 2003.

The JVS Campaign Actions
When grassroots activists in the JV created the Jordan Valley Solidarity (JVS) campaign, its local network of Palestinian grassroots community groups managed to garner material and non-material resources and organize actions to confront Israeli policies in the area. Building on existing *Sumud*, the campaign strengthened Palestinian steadfastness, while constructive resistance through building schools and community centers and developing livable infrastructure sustained and protected residents' existence in the valley.

Campaign members organized a wide range of actions to support villages building community schools, including in the Fasayil and Ka'abne communities. They relied on residents' skills to make hay-and-clay bricks for the buildings. Thus far, the JVS campaign has constructed six new schools and has expanded four preexisting schools. The JVS coordinator reports that these results have encouraged more residents to volunteer in the campaign's activities. Some have volunteered to teach in the schools not yet approved and funded by the Palestinian Ministry of Education. Meanwhile, external actors have provided the schools with necessary supplies. For example, Italian and French solidarity groups provided a bus to transport schoolchildren. After the Ras El-Ouja school was demolished, volunteers rebuilt it and renamed it the Vittorio Arrigoni School in honor of an Italian activist killed in Gaza and an Italian group that provided it with educational materials. The school now has the capacity for 25 students and its classes are taught by a volunteer from the village.

The JVS campaign has helped several communities by building roads and running water pipes to their villages. Its greatest achievement takes the form of the water networks its

---

21   Interview with the coordinator of the JVS campaign, in the north of the JV, June 2019.

42

activists have built, which were made possible when skilled volunteers secured relevant material resources such as plastic water pipelines for the campaign. The JVS coordinator notes that since the beginning of the campaign in 2003 they have provided the JV with more than 10 km of plastic water pipelines laid in more than ten Bedouin communities. Since farmers need the water, and the primary income of residents comes from agriculture, this achievement cannot be overstated. A farmer from Bardala village to the north of the JV explained that "the availability of the water enabled me to plant more land with watermelon, tomato, and zucchini. Thus, my income increased."[22] This small but vital success also strengthened residents' steadfastness and commitment to staying on their land, as confirmed in the interviews with the residents of the JV.

Since 2003, activists have mobilized local communities in the JV—such as Fasyel Al Fuqa, Maleh, and Humsa—to rebuild infrastructure destroyed by the Israeli army. Activists have also taught communities in the north Jordan Valley traditional building methods so they can build new structures or renovate buildings inexpensively using homemade, hay-and-clay bricks. They also plant trees to help preserve the land. With these strategies, JVS activists have acquired and harnessed internal resources to compensate for the scarcity of external resources caused by Israeli restrictions.

Most of the JV's residents have kinship relationships, which help them harness *Onah* to support one another. The communal trust and existing social capital that have been nourished and deepened represent a significant opportunity for any campaign. A farmer from the north of the Jordan valley reflected on this, commenting, "When we were together in Humsa community we were like a family. We stood with each other and supported each other despite their demolishing our tents six times in a month. But we rebuilt them, and we are here."[23] Effectively harnessing available social capital allowed campaign members to secure material resources such as labor and relevant skills.

JVS activists have successfully mobilized local communities around rebuilding structures destroyed by the Israeli occupation, helping the residents to stay on their land. In Al Makhoul community, they rebuilt their community after the Israeli occupation authorities demolished it. Furthermore, thanks to community members volunteering their time and energy, JV activists are able to better organize.

The primary obstacle to mobilization is posed by the long distances between communities across the 150-km length of the valley, where there is no public transportation available to Palestinians. Communication infrastructure exists only in towns and villages in Areas A and

---

22   Interview with an activist farmer from Bardala village to the north of the JV, 9 June 2019.

23   Interview with an activist from the north of the JV, 18 June 2019.

B, while the Israeli alternative is costly and could expose activists and their actions to surveillance by occupation forces.[24] Since there is no Palestinian communication infrastructure in Area C, people prefer dealing in person. Only a tiny minority of people in the JV community—usually the few Palestinian entrepreneurs whose businesses depend on the Israeli government's licensing—have internet access through Israeli mobile phones. To tackle this problem, activists have used decentralized tactics, including holding meetings in each community and using private cars to transport campaign members.

A further obstacle to mobilization is the dearth of local funding sources that would allow the campaign to sustain itself as an independent grassroots initiative. Very rarely have state bodies such as the PNA or external government actors come forward to fund a project that the campaign has undertaken. This problem has been addressed in part by mobilizing traditions and customs such as *Onah*, which encourages collaboration and sharing of resources and skills. *Onah* has been crucial in the JVS campaign as it has activated mutual assistance in the form of volunteer labor and skills-sharing to remedy the problem caused by long distances between communities. They have also relied on ad hoc financial support from individuals and organizations further afield.

The JVS campaign has continued its actions, harnessing the power of solidarity and the steadfastness of the JV's people, skillfully acquiring and deploying scarce local resources to achieve campaign objectives.

---

24   There is evidence to suggest that the Israeli occupation forces have discovered campaign actions as a result of Palestinian activists using Israeli SIM cards. Activists have even minimized using internet communication to avoid being discovered. In one case, the Israeli army arrested the coordinator of the Susya committee, presenting his recorded calls during the investigation. Also, in the Bab Al Shams action, they monitored the phone calls of the campaign organizers.

The Rebuilding Villages (RV) Campaign: 2013–2015

Geographic location	Occupied West Bank
Campaign period	2013–2015
Territorial scope	Area C
Beneficiaries	The residents of areas close to East Jerusalem, close to the Green Line/Armistice Line (1949), and close to the Israeli settlements
Amount of mobilized people	14,000–17,000
Number of campaign events	79
Scope of study	2013–2015

FIGURE 6. RV Campaign Geographical Locations

Location of the RV Campaign

The Rebuilding Villages (RV) campaign did not take place in one specific area like the SHH and JVS campaigns (see Figure 6). Instead, it targeted different areas close to East Jerusalem, areas close to the Green Line/Armistice Line (1949) (see Figure 3 on **page 29**), and settlements in Area C—areas where very few Palestinians are living because of Israeli policies that restrict their access. The locations were strategically selected in a plan to advance both the rights of individual Palestinians and the national cause. Sites were selected that were located on private land, making it more difficult for Israeli authorities to demolish villages without facing legal challenges. This strategy provided activists more time. The sites were also chosen to help create the geographical continuity needed for a unified Palestinian state. Whereas Palestinian movement in the SHH and the JV is possible though restricted, movement at the RV campaign sites is mostly limited or banned altogether by the occupying forces. Transporting materials and volunteers was therefore a considerable challenge for the campaign members, and it was extremely difficult to sustain a campaign under such conditions. Table 10 expounds on the locations, participants, and actions for each campaign site.

Table 10. A List of Villages Built in the Rebuilding Villages Campaign, Their Locations, and Actions

VILLAGE	LOCATION	NUMBER OF PARTICIPANTS	WHO WAS INVOLVED	NUMBER OF ACTIONS	DATE OF ACTION
Bab Al Shams	East of Jerusalem, E1 area	3000–3500	PSCC, PRCs, members from Political parties, residents of the villages nearby	10	January and March 2013
Al Manatir	Between Burin village and Brakha illegal settlement, south of Nablus	1000	Activists from the OPT, villagers from Burin village and the villagers of south of Nablus area, ISM, activists, Israeli activists. Bedouins living in E1 area, Al Quds university students	1	February 2, 2013
Ahfad Yunis	East of Abu Dies, East of Jerusalem	1500–2000	Residents from Abu Deis and Ezarya, PRCs, PSCC, STW and political parties	7	March 21–30, 2013
Kanaan	West of Hebron between the village of Sorif and Jab'a to the south of the West Bank	500	Activists from the OPT, residents from the villages southwest of Hebron, ISM activists and Israeli activists	1	June 8, 2013
Jerusalem Gate	East of Al Ezarya town, East of Jerusalem	5000–6000	Activists from the OPT, Jericho citizens, Bedouins living near by the Monastery	20	February 2014
Ein Hejle	North of the Dead Sea, southeast of Jericho	3000–4000	Activists from the OPT, Eizarya, Abu Dies towns, Bedouins living in E1 area, Al Quds university students	40	February and March 2015

Hardship and Repression of the Local Population

The Israeli government has escalated the building of Israeli settlements and the annexation of East Jerusalem and areas close to Israeli settlements within Area C. The names of these areas became popular slogans brought up regularly by Israeli politicians in election campaigns. For example, in the 2019 Israeli parliamentary elections, the right-wing parties called for the annexation of the entire JV by Israel. In fact, the annexation of Area C is no longer considered a matter for debate among the main political parties in Israel. The discussion now focuses on how it can be achieved without creating major international backlash. Furthermore, the Israeli settlers started to increase their activities in Area C by building houses and farms without permission from the Israeli government, actions which are deemed illegal even under Israeli law. The Israeli government ignored the fact that these are occupied areas by declaring some of them part of the Israeli state. After the announcement of the Trump administration's plan, which supported this declaration, settlers intensified their activities by establishing outposts at the edges of Palestinian communities. Recently, during the COVID-19 pandemic, the Israeli government has pushed to implement Trump's plan in Area C. All these activities limit the access of Palestinians to their land and prevent them from undertaking any construction work.

These areas are inhabited by the very few Palestinian Bedouins who are living there temporarily as part of their nomadic lifestyle. These Bedouins smuggle themselves and their sheep into these areas through the mountains. They often make their journeys during the night to avoid being discovered by the Israeli army. This shows the level of difficulty involved in people's movement that affects activism in these areas, including the acquisition of necessary material resources.

The RV campaign was established to counter Israeli policies in areas which the Israeli government declared annexed or considered to be part of Israel. The Popular Resistance Networks (PRNs) were the leading organizers. First, the campaign countered the Israeli occupation authorities to prevent land annexations. Second, it brought Palestinian families to live on these lands or helped them gain access to their land. The campaign was reactive in the sense that it was undertaken in response to Israeli authorities' declarations or intentions toward certain areas; however, the campaign was predominantly proactive in that it protected the land for the Palestinian people by working to prevent annexation and the eviction of residents from their communities. For example, the Bab Al Shams action was organized following the Israeli declaration to annex the E1 area and expand the Ma'ale Adumim settlement. The acquisition, adoption, and deployment of material and non-material resources were the key factors that led to the success of the campaign, and they happened despite all the Israeli oppressive measures on the ground. The constant Israeli surveillance of Palestinians' movement forced activists to be creative and adopt tactics that enabled them to safely transport material resources.

Rebuilding Villages Campaign and Its Actions

Palestinian grassroots activists began organizing the RV campaign in 2013. The larger goal of this campaign was to raise the visibility of land annexation and the building of Israeli settlements in the OPT. Its more specific, short-term goal was to rebuild Palestinian villages. Within two years, activists built eight villages: Bab Al Shams ("Gate of the Sun"), Ahfad Yunis, and Al Karama in 2013; and Jerusalem Gate, Ein Hejle, Al Manateer, Kaanan, and Zeyad Abu Ein in 2014.

Each village has a story behind its selection as a project site. For example, the rebuilding of Ahfad Yunis village coincided with President Barack Obama's visit to the OPT and Israel. It aimed to highlight the problems that Bedouin families face, such as forced displacement during the annexation of the greater East Jerusalem area. Similarly, after the US Secretary of State John Kerry had earlier proposed that Israel exercise control over the Jordan Valley, Ein Hejle village was rebuilt to signal to Kerry that there would be no final peace agreement with Israel without the JV forming part of the Palestinian state.

The campaign also sought to break the routine of weekly demonstrations in some villages against the annexation wall and the settlements. As the coordinator of the Popular Struggle Coordination Committee (PSCC) explained, the "RV campaign was seen as a qualitative transformation of the weekly demonstrations in the villages. Such a campaign is not about a one-day demonstration but about creating facts on the ground, on the land that is most likely to be annexed."[25]

An illustrative case is the construction of Bab Al Shams within E1, a 13-km^2 area of East Jerusalem. Building this village was the first action of the RV campaign, beginning on January 10, 2013. The name of the village was meant to inspire Palestinians' involvement as it was taken from the title of a novel written by the popular Lebanese author Elias Khouri. The novel describes the lives of Palestinian refugees and their attachment to their land. Bab Al Shams was the first village to be built by Palestinians since 1967. At the time of this writing, it consists of 25 tents, and 15 Palestinian Bedouin families live in the village. The land on which Bab Al Shams was constructed belongs to different Palestinian villages, including Abu Dis, Ezarya, and Ezayim. On July 1, 2020, Israeli Prime Minister Benjamin Netanyahu announced plans to annex the E1. This new situation might lead to the village's eviction.

---

25   Interview with the coordinator of the PSCC network, Ramallah, 16 June 2019.

Planning was a key tactic in the RV campaign. Grassroots activists started making plans a few weeks before construction began, and they relied on their extensive experience of organizing nonviolent actions in their villages over the previous decade and on the strong cross-village networks of activists. The biggest challenge was to amass resources, including labor and physical materials, and transport them without detection to sites designated by the Israeli army as a high security areas. To maintain secrecy and the element of surprise, activists adopted a tactic of decentralization when they recruited participants. RV activists always coordinated with the West Bank PRCs to agree on the number of people who would join the campaign from each village, and they would then arrange bus transport. This tactic worked because coordinators in each village were involved in campaign planning and carried part of the responsibility for recruiting volunteers.

Time is a crucial factor in the success or failure of this type of campaign because if the Israeli army discovers an action before construction begins, they can immediately prevent it. If they discover a village once the tents are built, it takes additional time and consideration to proceed with demolition. According to Israeli law, the procedures for preventing construction are different than those for dealing with buildings that already exist. Demolishing tents requires a legal process. The accompanying delay is key to ensuring the campaign's visibility and the momentum that helps mobilize more Palestinians to set up additional tents on the project site. This, in turn, creates greater dilemmas and challenges for the Israeli army.

At the start of the Bab Al Shams action, a few activists transported tents and building materials to the site three hours before the arrival of the other participants. Transporting the materials involved huge risks, and a bit of luck was needed to complete the transfer. An activist who participated in that action recounted that at one moment,

> My friend called me with a very soft and fearful voice saying: "They discovered our plan! There are two airplanes coming toward us. We have to hide under the trees." In the background, I hear another friend laughing loudly and then saying, "This is only a civil plane, and it has nothing to do with us!"[26]

Activists used their skills to establish the villages and divide the labor among themselves. In Bab Al Shams, around 500 activists arrived at the construction site in the E1 area at around five in the morning and built 25 tents within the first half hour. They then assigned tasks based on expertise. For example, a clinic was established and two doctors—Rajai and his brother—offered treatment to the volunteers who had become sick in the freezing winter temperatures. A media center was established, and skilled journalists volunteered reports on the campaign.

---

26   Interview with an activist from the Bab Al Shams campaign, 7 May 2019.

A mayor was elected to serve the needs of the village. Lawyers taught participants about their legal rights, and activists trained people in the practice of nonviolent resistance.

Press coverage prompted more Palestinians to join the effort. When the Israeli soldiers arrived, they were surprised not only by the village that had been established overnight but by the high level of organization already in place. The army closed the road and prevented anyone from accessing the village, which made transporting materials more difficult. However, it was too late for the army's measures to be effective since the activists had already built all the tents as planned. Soldiers, working under Israeli law, could not evict the villagers because activists had already opened a legal case and had built with consent on privately owned land.

The village lasted for two days before Netanyahu personally intervened to order its eviction, which was carried out early the next morning by over 1,000 soldiers. However, the court's ruling did not include the removal of materials such as the tents and the villagers' belongings:

> *We discovered later that the security agencies went to the home of the judge and asked him to change the order. And he allowed them to evacuate us under security reasons. But they did not demolish the tents. They just used their military order to take the people from the place. They did not have permission to destroy the tents.*[27]

The materials that remained in place were subsequently used by 15 families living in the E1 area. Despite the combined efforts of the Israeli military, legislature, and judiciary, the RV campaign succeeded in building a new village for Palestinian Bedouins in the E1 area of the West Bank.

The RV campaign, especially at Bab Al Shams, succeeded in postponing the building of 3,000 housing units planned for Israeli settlers. The campaign also generated international pressure on the Israeli government to not build in or annex the E1 area. It created unity among activists and helped make civil resistance more visible through the publicity it generated.

---

27   Ibid.

Chapter 3. Activists' Strategies for Determining the Kinds of Resources Needed

Chapter 2 showed how activists in the three campaigns managed to implement a wide range of tactics. It also indicated that the availability of material and non-material resources—and the ability to acquire or harness them—fostered the sustainability and momentum of the campaigns' actions.

Chapter 3 highlights the strategies adopted by campaign members to determine the different kinds of material and non-material resources needed for their campaigns. Tables 11, 12, and 13 (on pages 52–57) illustrate the three key strategies the campaigns used. The relationship between each key strategy and the type and nature of the resources they harnessed is a result of activists' practical innovations around the constraints imposed by the Israeli army. Activists cannot construct with expensive or highly visible materials, and they need to use equipment that is easy to carry, hide, and transport. For example, to build brick houses, they used bolster, hammers, hoes, hoists, spades, water levels, shovels, ladders, masonry, trowels, pickaxes, concrete mixers, and wheelbarrows. Such equipment is easy to hide, cheap, and relatively silent. Moreover, these manual tools avoid army detection. By using pickaxes instead of compressors to renovate caves, they prevented being heard by the army. Activists intentionally secured simple, manual equipment so that they could do the job without having their materials confiscated.

Table 11. Different Actions, and Types and Nature of Resources in the SHH Campaign

STRATEGIES USED TO HELP SPECIFY RESOURCES NEEDED	TYPES OF MATERIAL RESOURCES			
	BUILDING MATERIALS AND EQUIPMENT	IN-KIND CONTRIBUTIONS	FINANCIAL	HUMAN AND ORGANIZATIONAL RESOURCES
Identifying clear goals for the campaign	Shovels, axes, and hammers sand, cement, bricks	Food, drinks		Volunteer labor and skills in renovating caves and water wells Transnational networks Skills of media communication and documentation
	Plastic pipelines, solar panels	Food, drinks	Money	Volunteer labor and skills in making and building brick houses and in installing plastic water pipelines and solar panels
Relying on first-hand experience of communal live and its hardship	Building tools such as shovels, axes, and hammers	Hospitality	Money	Lawyers, technicians, engineers, and volunteers
Conducting face-to-face meetings	Equipment, building materials	Meeting venues, food and drinks	Money	Volunteers, skills

TYPES OF NON-MATERIAL RESOURCES		NATURE OF RESOURCES
SOCIAL RESOURCES	**CULTURAL RESOURCES**	
Social networks	In-depth knowledge of the communities *Onah, Ma'dood, Sumud,* semi-Bedouin traditions	Equipment that can be easily carried and moved without attracting unwanted attention from the army
Family relations		
Neighbors and acquaintances	Knowledge of Israeli legal context	Both material and non-material resources available in the SHH communities
		Can be installed easily, unlike galvanized steel pipes
		Easy to hide and move in case the Israeli army discovers them
Family relations, social networks	Experience in organizing nonviolent actions, semi-Bedouin traditions, *Onah, Ma'dood, Sumud*	Already available in the communities
		Ready to be harnessed by a campaign
Social networks, family relations	Local knowledge of the communities, semi-Bedouin traditions	Already available in the communities
		Ready to be harnessed by a campaign

Table 12. Different Actions, and Types and Nature of Resources in the JVS Campaign

STRATEGIES USED TO HELP SPECIFY RESOURCES NEEDED	MATERIAL RESOURCES			
	BUILDING MATERIALS AND EQUIPMENT	IN-KIND CONTRIBUTIONS	FINANCIAL	HUMAN AND ORGANIZATIONAL RESOURCES
Identifying clear goals for the campaign	Soil, hay for making bricks,	Food, drinks, tractors		Volunteer labor and skills in making and building hay-and-clay bricks Skills in media communication and documentation
	Plastic pipelines, wood, solar panels	Food, drinks, tractors	Money	Skills in installing plastic water pipelines and solar panels
Relying on first-hand experience of communal live and its hardship	Infrastructure materials, wood for community center, plastic pipelines	Hospitality	Money	Skills in infrastructure and building hay-and-clay bricks
Conducting face-to-face meetings	Wood	Venues, food and drinks	Money	Volunteers, skills, experience

NON-MATERIAL RESOURCES		NATURE OF RESOURCES
SOCIAL RESOURCES	CULTURAL RESOURCES	
Sumud, Ma'dood, Onah family relations and social networks External networks	In-depth knowledge of the communities' needs Knowledge of Israeli legal context	Materials that are available locally and can be deployed without attracting unwanted attention from the army Available non-material resource in the communities
		Easy to install Easy to hide and move in case the Israeli army discovers them
Social networks between different communities in the JV, family relations between the JV residents and neighborhood, acquaintance and trust	Experience in organizing nonviolent actions, in-depth knowledge in determining resources	Material and non-material resources available within the communities
Social networks, family relations	Semi-Bedouins traditions, local knowledge and know-how	Material and non-material resources available in the communities

Table 13. Different Actions, and Types and Nature of Resources in the RV Campaign

STRATEGIES USED TO HELP SPECIFY RESOURCES NEEDED	MATERIAL RESOURCES			
	BUILDING MATERIALS AND EQUIPMENT	IN-KIND CONTRIBUTIONS	FINANCIAL	HUMAN AND ORGANIZATIONAL RESOURCES
Identifying clear goals for the campaign	Tents, mobile houses, mattresses	Cars, vans, donkeys food, drinks, buses and vans, mules and houses	Money	Volunteers to put up the tents

Skills in installing plastic water pipelines and solar panels

Organizational networks Transnational networks

Skills in media communication and documentation |
| Relying on first-hand experience of communal live and its hardship | | | | |
| Conducting face-to-face meetings | | | | |

NON-MATERIAL RESOURCES		NATURE OF RESOURCES
SOCIAL RESOURCES	**CULTURAL RESOURCES**	
Social networks between activists and the residents of the area nearby the sites of the actions, friendship relations	Semi-Bedouin traditions; generosity, loyalty, hospitality	Material resources easy and fast to deploy Non-material resources available locally
	Knowledge of local geographic landscape Knowledge of Israeli legal context Experience and know-how Experience in organizing nonviolent actions	Do not need infrastructure, easy to hide and move in case the Israeli army discovers them Meet the needs of the families Non-material resources available locally
	Knowledge of local geographic and human landscape	Ease reaching the sites Help maintain the campaigns

Identifying Clear Goals for the Campaign

The first action adopted by actors across all the campaigns was to determine clear goals. The goal of the SHH campaign was to prevent the eviction of residents. For the JVS campaign, the goal was to rebuild houses and build essential infrastructure for local communities. Organizers of the RV campaign strove to highlight the danger of Israeli policies in Area C. The clarity of these goals helped grassroots activists determine which material resources were needed. For example, SHH activists decided that people needed alternative mid- to long-term housing to counter the impact of evictions, and so they helped dig, clean, and waterproof caves. When new caves were built, additional resources were required, including equipment that could be easily carried and moved without attracting attention from the army. Simple equipment such as shovels, axes, and hammers were secured from the residents, and additional labor and skills were acquired locally.

Similarly, in the JV, the clear goal of the campaign has been to protect people's existence there through constructive resistance. This has taken the form of building houses and community centers, laying roads and schools' water systems, and providing electricity. The members of the JVS campaign had to determine the kind of resources needed, including sand for making bricks, plastic pipelines, wood, and solar panels, as well as skills such as brickmaking. The cultural resources they mobilized included the resilience of the residents and their knowledge about organizing and campaigning.

In the RV campaign, clear goals helped activists decide to build tents because they were easy and fast to put up. When they searched for providers of the goods they needed, they relied on their network relationships with Palestinian NGOs and the PNA to provide the tents. The planning process therefore had an impact on the implementation of the campaign's actions.

First-Hand Experience of Communal Life and Its Hardships

In the SHH and JVS campaigns, organizers are residents of these communities. Their first-hand experience of hardship helped them determine what needed to be fixed and what kinds of resources were needed to do this. They effectively made use of an organic needs-based assessment process. Furthermore, activists' prior experience in popular resistance—through organizing nonviolent actions in their communities and their involvement in past campaigns—enhanced their ability to identify and assess resource needs. Activists' in-depth knowledge of their community, their intimate relationship with fellow residents and familiarity with their needs and problems, and their knowledge of the history of local resistance have together facilitated an understanding of the kinds of material and non-material resources on which a campaign can rely. This is especially true in smaller communities where organizers have relatives and where people trust and communicate with one another.

At the same time, it is important to note that, even when needs are known and the list is narrowed down to key priorities, resources are often inadequate. For example, the PRCs involved in these campaigns needed lawyers to help in the struggle to prevent house demolitions and secure master plans.[28] They also needed technical specialists to install renewable energy sources such as solar panels and wind turbines. In the SHH, electrical engineers from Comet-ME, an Israeli–Palestinian organization, conducted the needs assessment for renewable energy in the whole area. Civil engineers have also been required to support alternative planning processes and present maps that will serve as master plans for communities in Area C. The coordinator of Bab Al Shams said that the first step toward building the village was to choose a private parcel of land, and this meant that they needed to consult an Israeli cartographer. This expert also had to have access to the official land ownership records. His work helped determine precisely which piece of land the community could use. In the JV, activists made use of local knowledge to determine that tents were not suitable in the area's hot weather, and they opted instead to use hay-and-clay bricks.

When this kind of local knowledge is absent, resources can be of no real benefit even if they are available or are donated with good intentions. For example, in the SHH where people were choosing to live in caves, the US organization Action Against Hunger provided people with tents without consulting them about their needs. The organization's representative explained that they only had one kind of tent, and so they distributed this resource even though it was redundant in that location. This points to the need for the campaign members that have first-hand knowledge of local conditions to be involved in decisions about whether and what resources external actors should provide.

The types of material resources used in the three campaigns were identified based on the communities' needs and the decisions of the residents. In the SHH and JVS campaigns, homes have been built to meet the needs of families and plans have accommodated the cultural context in which communities are structured around family relationships. The PRCs in the SHH and the JV were formed around different family branches; therefore, it was easy to map the community and its needs rapidly. Still, family heads had to be consulted regarding the kinds of materials they needed because they enjoy authority and are considered highly knowledgeable about their communities. Also, members of the PRCs—who were often from the communities where campaigns were implemented—were very familiar with the sets of skills, expertise, and experience that the residents of each community possessed. Activists relied on close relationships with the community members to assess available human and organizational resources and to recruit people with the appropriate skillsets for each project. In the RV campaign, the PRCs established mechanisms such as visiting the project sites with

---

28   The master plan is a formal recognition by the Israeli civil administration that Palestinian villagers are permitted to build in the delineated areas. No more than 10 out of 180 villages located in Area C have a master plan.

professional consultants, conferring with residents, and holding meetings with domestic and international actors interested in helping the campaign. This process helped organizers choose the kinds of materials they needed and taught them to acquire these resources depending on the availability of local expertise and experience.

Conducting Face-to-Face Meetings

Because of the lack of communication infrastructure, many face-to-face meetings were held with village councils, heads of communities, and local project committees to identify future construction sites and the material and non-material resources needed. These meetings were crucial in helping activists divide the tasks involved in securing or harnessing resources among the PRCs and the local councils. When activists decided to build a school as part of the SHH campaign in one of the communities, a series of meetings with the project committee helped identify the site of the school as well as the necessary resources. Campaign organizers then reached out to the residents to find a local contributor who could donate a piece of land where the school could be built. They also visited a committee member's relative in Yatta who was working in the presidential office and provided an opportunity to ask the PNA for financial support. The committee also determined the skills and voluntary labor needed to build the school and then secured them from among the residents.

In the JV, similar meetings enabled activists to identify and source the resources needed to build community centers, schools, and essential infrastructure. However, in the RV campaign, face-to-face meetings brought together activists who were members of different PRNs, and they worked collectively to figure out the material resources required to build villages at several locations. The face-to-face meetings format is extremely valuable to a campaign. The diverse experience of activists across the OPT can inform decisions about the types and sources of resources needed for each action.

This chapter analyzed the processes and mechanisms involved in determining the resources needed for the campaigns. It showed that clear goals for the campaign, first-hand experience, and face-to-face meetings are crucial factors in determining these resources. Making clear goals in order to determine necessary resources is the primary step toward developing appropriate strategies to acquire and harness those resources. The next chapter will address the second step after deciding what resources are needed, namely, the process of acquiring or harnessing the material and non-material resources needed to carry out the campaigns.

Chapter 4. How Material and Non-material Resources Were Acquired or Harnessed

As Table 1 in Chapter 1 demonstrates, the resources generated for the campaigns can be divided into categories of material and non-material resources. In the nonviolent campaigns surveyed here, some of the materials generated were internally harnessed with the help of domestic actors, while others were acquired from external actors or with their help (see Tables 14, 15, and 16). Campaign organizers have generated resources by seeking donations through individual contributions and fundraising, and by charging for goods and services. Sand, cement, and materials to renovate wells and caves were acquired by activists with the help of external actors. In turn, non-material, socio-cultural resources were already available and could be harnessed for the campaign's purposes as activists prepared for, mobilized, launched, and sustained their local activism—resources that included local knowledge, *Sumud*, *Ma'dood*, *Onah*, and semi-Bedouin traditions, including communal loyalty and trust, a sense of belonging and hospitality, personal and familial relationships, and the authority of the heads of families that supported the campaigns.

This chapter focuses on the kinds of material and non-material resources campaign actors managed to generate in the three specific nonviolent campaigns.

Table 14. Types of Resources in the SHH Campaign Acquired Through Domestic or External Sources

	SHH CAMPAIGN RESOURCES	
	MATERIAL RESOURCES	**NON-MATERIAL RESOURCES**
Domestic Actors: Internally Harnessed and/or Harnessed with Grassroots Help	Building materials, equipment, volunteer labor, money, skills in building, food, drinks, meeting venues, plastic water pipelines, solar panels, sand, and cement	In-depth knowledge of the area, *Onah*, *Ma'dood*, *Sumud*, the know-how needed to organize nonviolent actions, semi-Bedouin traditions, communal loyalty and trust, a sense of belonging and hospitality, personal and familial relationships, authority of the heads of families
External Actors: Externally Acquired or Acquired with External Help	Building materials, money, plastic water pipelines, solar panels	Knowledge/skills related to documentation of nonviolent actions, capacity-building training, solidarity, film production, writing press releases

61

Table 15. Types of Resources in the JVS Campaign Acquired Through Domestic or External Sources

	JVS CAMPAIGN RESOURCES	
	MATERIAL RESOURCES	NON-MATERIAL RESOURCES
Domestic Actors: Internally Harnessed and/or Harnessed with Grassroots Help	Hay-and-clay bricks, infrastructure material resources, plastic pipelines, solar panels, skills in making hay-and-clay bricks	In-depth knowledge of the area, *Onah, Ma'dood, Sumud,* the know-how required to organize nonviolent actions, semi-Bedouin traditions, communal loyalty and trust, a sense of belonging and hospitality, personal and familial relationships, authority of the heads of families
External Actors: Externally Acquired or Acquired with External Help	Money, educational tools for schools, a school bus, plastic pipelines, and solar panels	Knowledge in documenting, nonviolent actions and acts of repression, capacity-building training, solidarity, film production, writing press releases

Table 16. Types of Resources in the RV Campaign Acquired Through Domestic or External Sources

	RV CAMPAIGN RESOURCES	
	MATERIAL RESOURCES	NON-MATERIAL RESOURCES
Domestic Actors: Internally Harnessed and/or Harnessed with Grassroots Help	Tents, cars, buses, gasoline, money, experience in nonviolent actions	The know-how required to organize actions and set up tents, skill to write press releases
External Actors: Externally Acquired or Acquired with External Help	Money	Knowledge about land ownership (whether it is a private or state land), knowledge about Israeli laws, the know-how required to organize disciplined nonviolent actions

Non-material Resources: Social and Cultural Resources

This study defines non-material resources as social capital in the form of social and cultural resources. Social resources include family relations, neighborhood acquaintances, and trust. Cultural resources include the traditions of semi-Bedouin people, *Onah, Ma'dood, Sumud,* local knowledge, activists' experience, and the know-how needed for organizing and campaigning (see Table 3 on **page 10**). These kinds of non-material resources were harnessed from domestic and external actors. The interviews for this study highlight the importance of social capital and inform the discussion below.

Family Relations and Communal Trust

Family relations are the strong familial bonds between family members and comprise the organic networks that existed among the residents of the SHH and, separately, among the

62

residents of the JV. These familial ties form the basis of social organization in semi-Bedouin communities, which are structured around family hierarchy and tribal laws in the absence of more formal organizational structures.

Family relations were a primary non-material resource that activists harnessed for the purpose of the campaign. As insiders living in these communities, activists knew the social values of their communities and used this knowledge of semi-Bedouin culture to unite the campaigns' adherents and secure volunteers' participation. For example, when women needed more space in their homes and caves, as well as electricity and water, family members and neighbors participated in renovating caves and installing renewable energy. When shepherds needed access to grazing areas for their sheep, volunteers from their families joined the campaign to accompany them. Residents of Yatta who owned land in the SHH were also supportive of the campaign and helped their relatives gain access to their land, thereby making it more likely that they themselves would be able to live on it in the future. The residents of the SHH and Yatta have become key constituencies for the campaigns.

Family relations, neighborhood acquaintances, and communal trust were used strategically to generate material resources. Family relations and communal trust allowed activists to communicate and meet with community residents in person and secure their commitment to campaign goals and actions. For example, while conducting interviews for this study, the author noticed how easy it was to enter any house in the communities when accompanied by the campaign organizers because of the existing family relations and communal trust. In general, each community in the SHH and the JV consists of one family; sometimes more than one community can consist of the same family. This made most residents supportive of the campaigns and helped activists recruit volunteer labor to build brick houses, make hay-and-clay bricks, and provide other skills and financial support. Family relations also allowed activists to tap into the full range of resources available in the communities.

From the activists' point of view, all these family-based communities were living with the same grievances. By framing individual threats to family members as collective threats to the whole community, activists were able to use social capital to harness material resources. This increased the residents' commitment to volunteer their time, skills, and labor to the campaigns. For example, whenever the Israeli authorities demolish a resident's house, the community supports the owner by helping to rebuild it because of their familial bonds. Family relations as a social resource were at the core of mobilizing community members and facilitating their collaboration. An activist from the north of the JV explained that "when the settlers made obstacles for us to reach land adjacent to the settlement, the family members were the first to protect the land. My brother talked to the family members and they were all motivated to join in cultivating the land."[29] Family relations turned whole communities into active participants in the campaigns' actions.

Communal trust, which is at the heart of residents' support for campaign actions, is inherent in the semi-Bedouin culture of the SHH and JV communities, which is based on loyalty to the tribe and the family. By building on these relationships and a sense of shared threat, activists won the trust of residents, not only because they were the members of these communities but also because their actions demonstrated that they were ready to make personal sacrifices to solve community problems. Moreover, the involvement of locals themselves in actions and decision making fostered trust among all involved.

Semi-Bedouin Traditions

Grassroots activists have also used semi-Bedouin traditions to mobilize domestic material resources. Semi-Bedouin traditions form the rhythm of community members' behavior. The residents live simple lives in tents or caves and withstand a life of hardship. They are attached to their land and communities with strong internal solidarity.

One of their traditions is *Onah,* which is a traditional practice in the Palestinian countryside whereby people work together to harvest their fields. It plays a role in creating harmonious community relations and mitigating social differences. It is often used to provide support for elderly people during the harvest season, and it is reflected in volunteers joining activities in the mosques and assisting at various social occasions. Farmers can also call for meetings in the house of the head of the community and ask attendees to come together with their family members.

In recent years, the *Onah* practice has been used to recruit volunteers to protect farmers from settlers' attacks, to organize work in the fields at harvest time, and to rebuild houses destroyed under the occupation's policies. SHH residents have helped each other not only with construction and farming but also with grazing their sheep and traveling in groups to protect each other while completing these tasks. As shown in Table 8 (on **page 19**), cultural resources such as *Onah* helps harness different kinds of material resources such as money, building materials, and in-kind contributions. *Onah* also fosters internal solidarity among community residents. As one activist pointed out, *Onah* means "you have to support your neighbor with everything you can, and you cannot rest while your neighbor is not resting."[30]

---

29   Interview with an activist farmer from the north of the JV, 14 July 2019.

30   Interview with an activist farmer, north of the JV, Hadidya village, 9, June 2019.

64

The communities in the JV and the SHH are very traditional, and therefore activists have used traditions, customs, and religious values to inspire people to donate material resources. Activists have promoted the idea that volunteering and donating for the campaign are a form of goodness and communal philanthropy and that helping your neighbor has social value. Another semi-Bedouin tradition is *Ma'dood*, which means that each community member contributes material resources for the community's use. These contributions have been used to provide public services—including schools and roads—and to renovate or build new power grids. An activist from Al Mufaqara offered an example of this process when he explained that "Each resident of Al Mufaqara community was providing material resources to build the mosque despite the fact that the Israeli soldiers have destroyed it twice. It was the first concrete building in a community where its residents have been living in caves."[31]

Furthermore, activists relied on the cultural resource of *Sumud* as a tactic to generate material resources. *Sumud* is the cornerstone of most of the campaigns' actions because it represents the ability of the residents to bear the hardship of their lives, stand up for their rights, and pool their resources together to organize nonviolent resistance. This study finds that most residents of the SHH and the JV have relatives in cities and towns such as Yatta, Tubas, and Jericho. Some of them own land in the cities and they could easily move and live there. Because of their *Sumud*, they chose to stay put, organize the campaigns, and challenge the occupation despite having opportunities for other living arrangements. This resilience and determination was also reflected in the interviews, as one SHH resident stated: "I prefer to live in this cave without electricity with my 18 children rather than going to live in the city of Yatta, which is a nearby town, with all the amenities."[32] *Sumud* has become a source of resilient mobilization that pushes local people to volunteer in the campaigns. It strengthens the communities and increases their commitment to help the campaigns, including with necessary material resources.

The Know-How of Expert Activists
Activists' experiences and knowledge about how to organize nonviolent actions were used as shareable cultural, non-material resources in the three campaigns. The know-how of expert activists helped increase residents' participation in campaign actions. This specifically happened after 2002, when the residents of communities affected by the segregation wall started to organize collective direct actions against the confiscation of their agricultural fields. A group of activists emerged from these communities who, over the previous decade, had gained considerable experience and knowledge in organizing, overcoming Israeli repression,

---

31   Interview with the head of Al Mufaqara, one of the SHH communities, 5 May 2019.

32   Interview with an activist from the Al Mufaqara community, 5 May 2019.

and building vibrant national and international networks. Palestinians referred to these activists as "expert activists" or "the Wall resisters."

Their knowledge of activism proved to be invaluable in later campaigns. In 2013, Al-Makhoul village, to the north of the JV, was demolished and everyone was evicted, but when experienced activists intervened and stayed there, families started to return and together they rebuilt it. These interventions transform *Sumud* and everyday resistance into more open and direct collective actions. This happened in the SHH campaign, particularly in the villages of Susya and Al Mufaqara. Activists gained an understanding of legal processes from their long-term experience on the ground. Israeli activists also helped them access relevant legal information and lawyers, allowing Palestinian activists to deploy their legal acumen to postpone and sometimes prevent house demolitions. Activists also used their expertise to negotiate with residents and domestic actors and network with external actors to acquire material resources. The knowledge and skills of expert activists helped campaigns build unity, maintain their momentum, and overcome challenges faced by previous campaigns.

Local Knowledge

Another cultural resources deployed by activists is local knowledge, which is understood as in-depth knowledge of communities, their history, and their residents' lives, including their grievances, hopes, and demands. This local knowledge was used to develop and implement campaigns that aimed to acquire the types of resources needed to address the specific needs of the communities.

Campaign organizers were themselves residents whose grievances stemmed directly from the Israeli occupation and violations of their rights. Some activists were arrested, while others had their homes demolished. Activists were rooted in the culture of their troubled communities and were legitimized by their sharing in group suffering and destiny. Activists' biographical experiences provided them deep insights into the residents' motives and needs, as well as their cultural and organizational resources.

Activists' deep familiarity with community grievances helped them determine the kinds of materials needed and the campaign actions that were feasible given the chances of acquiring and harnessing resources and their relevance to addressing existing grievances. Activists' residency in these communities also enabled them to have an in-depth knowledge of relevant traditions and customs, which helped them recruit volunteers for campaign actions and secure financial resources, while their practical knowledge of activism equipped them with skills to transport and hide material resources in the communities.

On more than one occasion in the JV and the SHH, the author saw how activists' intimate knowledge of communities was used for the benefit of the campaigns. One day, the SHH community was energized to build a plastic water pipeline network after a local activist gave a speech about the effects of water shortages on their crops. He detailed how these problems could be solved by installing plastic pipes. Many people volunteered to implement his solution. Similarly, in the JV, activists' knowledge was used to develop plans for solving their problems. For example, their detailed knowledge of underground water and the Israeli water networks enabled them to solve water shortages by installing plastic pipelines and securing local labor to dig wells. Because of their past experiences, activists had the skills to hide plastic pipelines to avoid their confiscation by the Israeli army. In general, they had to skills to manage material resources effectively, as one activist explained:

> My village has 400 inhabitants, and we are all from one family. This has allowed us to communicate with everyone without problems and establish harmonious relations with the people. Such relations with local people make for a healthy situation in which we can mobilize the resources from our communities. Our knowledge is enriched by living here. It is the base we rely on to generate and use material resources.[33]

Activists' knowledge of the problems and grievances of the residents were used directly in developing plans for acquiring material resources from domestic and external actors. Activists had this local knowledge because many of them were insiders and community residents themselves, and this in turn enabled them to establish trust and strong relationships with community members and other networks of popular resistance.

Figure 7 summarizes the use of non-material resources to harness and acquire material resources for the ultimate goal of each campaign.

Material Resources

The following section explains how various non-material resources were employed to secure specific material resources to build and renovate homes and infrastructure. In Chapter 1, Figure 2 illustrated that non-material resources are used to harness and acquire material resources. Figure 7 further develops the concept of Figure 2, showing the relationship between each of the non-material and material resources that will be discussed in greater detail below.

---

33 Interview with the coordinator of Susya village, December 2019.

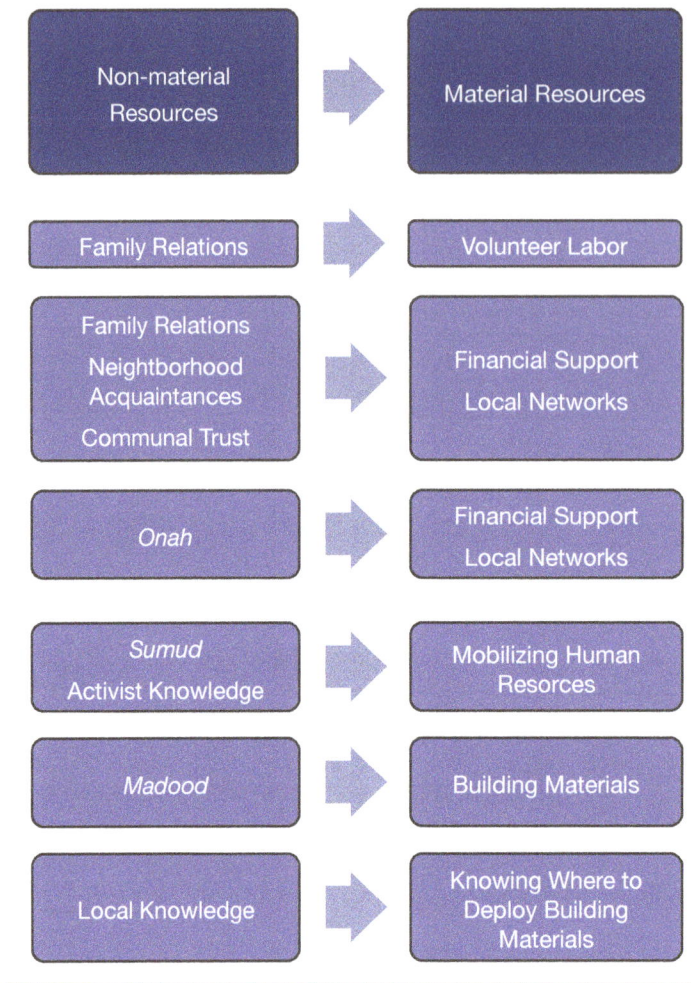

FIGURE 7. How Non-material Resources Harnessed Material Resources

Financial Contributions and Proceeds

Campaign actors managed to generate financial resources through monetary donations, grants, and the sale of goods and services. These financial contributions were raised internally from the residents of the communities themselves and, with the help of the PRCs and PRNs, from the PNA and Palestinian NGOs. The PRCs and PRNs also helped secure financial support from external actors, such as INGOs. Through the PRNs and local councils, campaign organizers managed to apply for external grants that, in turn, allowed them to secure the building materials needed for the campaigns' actions, such as plastic pipelines and solar panels.

In the SHH, activists secured donations from domestic and external actors that allowed them to obtain most of the building materials needed to rebuild demolished houses and to build schools, electrical power grids, and water pipeline networks. Domestic Palestinian actors such as the PNA and its different ministries—including the ministries of local government, agriculture, and education—financially supported project committees and the local councils. For example, prior to 2004, Al Tuwani's residents secured $38,000 from the presidential office of Yasser Arafat. In the JV, activists attracted financial donations from Palestinian NGOs, including the Ma'an Development Center, to help build water networks, community centers, and houses.

Fundraising from external actors also increased when activists intensified their nonviolent actions, including protests and sit-ins at the entrances to their villages. Israeli repression of some communities backfired and increased the visibility of Palestinian suffering and their nonviolent response. The JVS campaign also raised funds from external actors following the escalation of house demolitions. For example, they have been able to attract monetary and non-monetary resources from the UK's Brighton JVS group, Machsom Watch, the L'Association France Palestine Solidarité (AFPS), the Israeli Committee Against House Demolitions, the Stop the Wall campaign, and the Popular Struggle Coordination Committee (PSCC).

Media coverage helped activists network with NGOs and international solidarity actors, providing the campaigns with financial support to maintain momentum. In the context of the campaigns, the media played two key roles: first, it served as an outside asset—material and non-material—that attracted the attention of external actors who provided the campaigns with needed resources. Second, it disseminated information about the campaigns and thus played an advocacy role on behalf of the residents. For example, in 1999 Oxfam intervened in the SHH after the media covered the eviction of the 15 Palestinian communities. At this time, access to media was through newspapers, radio, and television. Social media networks were not yet present and email lists played a very limited role.

In 2002, the establishment of the International Solidarity Movement (ISM) by Palestinian and international activists connected external actors with domestic activists in the SHH and the JV and helped international activists make frequent visits to the campaigns on the ground and thus better understand the local situation. This increased the level of external financial support that was provided either directly to the PRCs or via the PSCC. When residents were evicted or had other rights violated, it would trigger a snowball effect of growing support through their networks with international actors. These violations attracted interest and con-cern from solidarity groups, and activists were able to keep them informed. After activists networked with these solidarity groups, they were able to translate their solidarity into much-needed financial resources.

Both the survey and the interviews with local activists conducted as part of this study show that networking with external groups played an important role in securing financial donations. In fact, external actors helped further expand funding networks. For example,

Israeli peace activists played a crucial role in building networks between SHH activists and international actors. As a result, more monetary resources from international actors were generated to support campaign actions. The SHH campaign coordinator emphasized that "the Israeli groups were the first to visit the SHH and they were the ones who mobilized Operation Dove [an Italian organization recruiting volunteers to conflict zones to monitor and document human rights violations] to come to the area."[34] Since 2004, the ISM, the Ecumenical Accompaniment Program in Palestine and Israel (EAPPI), the Christian Peacemakers Team (CPT), and Operation Dove have had a constant presence in the SHH. Those external actors helped acquire financial support through advocacy for these campaigns. In turn, their involvement attracted the attention of other international solidarity groups, such as Assopace and Civil Service International, which brought in more support—and additional funds—to local committees.

The activists in the RV campaign secured all the material resources they needed from a combination of domestic and external sources. The campaign was organized by local activists along with the PSCC's staff members, who were more skilled and experienced than the members of the PRCs in the JV and SHH. The PSCC also has stronger networks with other national and international actors than the PRCs, thanks to its structure, organization, and staff members. In the JVS and SHH campaigns, activists relied on media coverage and the skills of Palestinian and international activist groups while activists in the RV campaigns relied on skills from within their own communities.

Monetary Donations
Monetary donations in the SHH and JVS campaigns were provided by locals, especially at the beginning when residents were the only source of support and campaign actions depended on the help of grassroots activists. The residents donated money to support the construction of public infrastructure or services, such as schools and water pipeline networks, and the nature of these projects encouraged local generosity. The residents of the SHH and the JV showed great commitment to providing monetary resources, and campaign organizers used constructive resistance to keep the residents motivated and encourage continued donations. Residents' generosity and donations increased when the campaigns focused on public services. Stories from the JVS and SHH campaigns reflected residents' enthusiasm for solving their local problems and challenges through their own donations despite their existing hardship. The commitment of residents was aided by their semi-Bedouin traditions such as *Ma'dood*. Their donations were not limited to public services but were also provided to cover the cost of rebuilding demolished houses. Though donations mostly came from families living in the SHH and the JV, some came from their extended family living in other

---

34   Interview with the coordinator of the SHH campaign, south of the West Bank, 1 May 2019.

Palestinian towns. This type of financial support from campaign actors came without conditions, which meant that campaign actors could use the money to fund activities in the way they themselves deemed necessary and effective.

In the SHH and JVS campaigns, local activists had neither internet access nor the skills needed to produce online content and communication, write grant proposals, or carry out online fundraising and crowdfunding. In rare best-case scenarios, residents of the SHH had mobile phones but no internet access, as one activist explained: "In 1999, we have only two mobile phones in the SHH" and there were no land-lines to provide an internet connection.[35] Because there was no electricity either, activists had to travel about an hour to Yatta to charge their phones. The Israeli government prohibited 3G mobile bandwidth until 2016, and a lack of technical skills and of English proficiency in these communities prevented activists from generating external financial resources through fundraising initiatives aimed at international groups.

Residents gave financial support directly to activists they knew personally so that they could buy building materials and other necessary equipment.

This problem was amplified in the JV due to the dispersion of its communities across a large area. Poor infrastructure was one of the important motivators behind residents' donations to campaign actions that were spearheaded by experienced local activists. Residents of the SHH and the JV gave financial support directly to activists they knew personally so that they could buy building materials and other necessary equipment and tools.

Monetary donations were also acquired from domestic and external actors. Activists were able to secure financial support from others after they had gradually built networks with domestic and external actors. For example, following the dramatic events of November 1999 in the SHH, Palestinian and international organizations became more involved in the campaign, resulting in an increase in external financial contributions. Activists were able to acquire monetary resources after external actors such as Ta'ayush, ISM, and Operation Dove visited the SHH and the JV. The residents and activists were able to network with them, and they became allies and partners in their campaigns. The financial support, which came from these solidarity groups, was provided without conditions, and activists were free to use it in their campaigns as they saw fit.

This financial support covered printing materials, fines, bail costs, and legal defense fees for arrested activists, and it was also used to contest demolition orders in the Israeli courts. Donated funds were managed by the PRC and disbursed according to the current needs of the campaign. However, in the SHH and JVS campaigns these resources were limited

---

35   Interview with an activist from SHH, 5 May 2019.

because they were provided by individuals and small solidarity groups. By contrast, the RV campaign was able to generate sufficient financial resources by drawing on contributions from a wide range of actors: individual Palestinians, the Palestinian government, and international organizations.

In summary, activists generated money from residents and international solidarity groups who provided unconditionally and gave directly to PRCs and PRNs. Moreover, some financial support was offered by NGOs, INGOs, and the PNA to purchase specific materials for the campaigns, including building materials, plastic pipelines, and crushed rocks suitable for making and paving roads.

Grants

Financial contributions were not limited to donations from domestic and external actors; they were also generated through formal grants mainly provided by NGOs, INGOs, and the PNA. This happened when the campaigns gained media attention, built networks with external actors, and—following the establishment of the PRNs and the local councils—started reaching out to various Palestinian NGOs and INGOs to apply for grants on their behalf. This arrangement was needed because the campaign actors and the villages' councils did not have the appropriate skills for writing grant proposals. Once grants were approved, local NGOs and INGOs used them to buy necessary building materials and provided them directly to the campaign actors. Eventually, the PRNs built their staff members' skills and acquired appropriate legal status so that they could apply for grants themselves. For example, the PSCC registered as an NGO and applied for grants from a wide range of domestic and international actors. Table 17 shows the kinds of grants the PSCC applied for. Unlike the unconditional financial support offered by the residents and solidarity groups, financial assistance won through grants was restricted to the projects described in the submitted proposals.

Table 17. Examples of Projects Applied for by the PSCC

PROJECTS WHERE FUNDING WAS APPLIED FOR BY THE PSCC TO SUPPORT CAMPAIGNS	PROVIDER/CONTRIBUTOR	USE OF FUNDS
Building brick houses in the SHH	The French Consulate	All the grants were for building materials
Beyond the Wall project	EU Commission, in partnership with SCI	Building materials, non-material resources
Human rights and resilience	Spanish Agency for International Development Cooperation	Material and non-material resources

PRNs were also able to acquire funds from the Palestinian government. For example, the PSCC received a grant of $13,000 a month for four years. Similarly, the local councils were able to receive funds from the Palestinian government that were mainly used to buy the infrastructure materials needed for digging roads, installing water pipe networks, and building schools.

Local councils were able to apply for grants from the Palestinian government and to receive money from the PNA. Many international aid organizations and Palestinian NGOs applied for grants in partnership with the local councils to support the campaigns. The local councils therefore benefited from their existing social networks as well as from their newly established relationships with domestic and external organizations. The PRNs' grants were used to build campaign capacities in different areas such as documentation, media and communication, and human rights, and they empowered activists to control actions on the ground and to undermine the power of the army. This created a strong image of popular resistance that has impressed Palestinians and helped mobilize them to participate in demonstrations. It has also enabled activists to generate additional material resources.

Before the establishment of PRNs such as the PSCC, local activists had neither substantial financial resources nor the skills needed to manage large grant projects, which would normally have been implemented directly by Oxfam or run by other INGOs and implemented through local partners. Funders will not commit resources to organizations that lack adequate administrative and reporting capacity—something that grassroots organizers usually lack. Therefore, activists prioritize non-monetary resources that can be secured from Palestinian actors which do not require organizational reporting capacity. At the same time, non-monetary resources—such as bricks, cement, and water pipelines—can be used to increase the trust between activists and domestic and international providers on the one hand and between activists and residents on the other where the latter are direct beneficiaries of the campaign's end-products (e.g., housing, water systems, solar panels, and other infrastructure for their villages). The SHH and JVS campaigns are long-term and have been running for 20 and 16 years, respectively, at the time of this writing. Grant management can lead to fractures and disagreements, and while this might be of little consequence in short-term campaigns, it is certain to derail attempts to organize in the long-term. Activists reported that the Youth of Sumud campaign in the SHH and also the JVS campaign witnessed disputes as a result of grants received from the PNA and INGOs. To some extent it also caused challenges for the PRNs when they received grants from the PNA (discussed further in Chapter 8).

Sale of Goods and Services
Activists have sold goods and services to visitors to raise funds for the campaigns. Goods include t-shirts, art, food, and embroidered items such as scarves, daypacks, and cushion covers. Services include lodging for visitors and organizing tours. Visitors on these tours tend

to include Palestinians from universities and cities as well as international activists and groups who come on educational tours to see rural communities.

When media coverage brought solidarity groups to the SHH and JV communities, grassroots activists established women's embroidery cooperatives that produced a variety of embroidered products for sale. Those products were sold directly to the solidarity groups who resold them in their home countries to generate money for the nonviolent campaigns in Palestine. These initiatives have helped maintain campaign momentum in two different ways: First, the women producing the embroidery have been encouraged to participate because the campaigns have opened new markets for their goods. Second, the income gained has been divided so that it provides the women with greater economic stability while also generating money for the campaigns.

In both the SHH and JV, the profits from selling homemade food to visitors is divided between the women who cook and the PRCs, which use these funds to support their nonviolent activities. Um Jamil, who is responsible for the Fasayel Community Center in the JV, explains that "I cook food for the solidarity groups when they come to visit us. I used to give five percent of the income to the committee and with the rest I manage the cooking with other women and buy the ingredients."[36] While the generation of resources through sales has been an effective strategy in the SHH and JVS campaigns, no similar schemes were used to generate material resources in the RV campaign.

The activists reported that hosting Palestinians and international visitors in their communities also generated financial support for the nonviolent campaigns. According to one activist, when the PRCs networked with solidarity groups, they began receiving delegations that would stay in these communities, sometimes for days or weeks, with each person paying $20 per night for lodging in the community centers and family houses in the JV villages. The market for goods and services has thus increased due to the advocacy of international and Israeli activists on behalf of the SHH and JV communities. Income from hosting delegations was paid directly to the local committees and subsequently divided between the PRCs and the host families.

In-Kind Contributions
In-kind contributions, such as giving out goods and volunteering services, were another type of material resource that activists harnessed from within their communities. Contributions such as the use of homes, offices, cars, food and drink, tractors, and donkeys were extremely important to the campaigns. In the 1990s, the SHH and JV communities had no public buildings (e.g., libraries, sport centers, cultural facilities) that their residents could utilize. Since there was not even a mosque where people could gather or hold meetings, activists' homes became *de facto* meeting places, as one activist commented: "I do not remember one night

---

36   Interview with the head of the Fasayel village women center, 18 May 2019.

where I had dinner with my family alone. There were always other activists in my house. My wife was happy to offer hospitality to the activists."[37]

Food and drink for the participants who came to discuss nonviolent resistance activities were provided by activists' families. Women were cooking food for laborers and other activists as they worked. In the RV campaign, the PSCC offered its premises as a venue for meetings and as a place to prepare materials for the campaign. Printing materials, laptops, cameras, banners, leaflets, stationery, and loudspeakers were provided by PRNs and by B'Tselem, a Jerusalem–based human rights organization.

In the SHH campaign, meetings for campaign organizers were held in the houses of residents. These places offered intimacy, familial connections, friendship, and opportunities to exchange and share information and develop planning capacity. They all aided activists in securing building materials and equipment from locals. When activists met face-to-face in each other's houses, they would sit down and discuss the availability of house-building equipment in the community and who could contribute what kinds of tools. In the absence of other means of communication, activists' houses became the only meeting spaces where residents could meet easily and comfortably to plan for actions. Figure 8, on the next page, shows the relationship between the material resources that constituted in-kind contributions to the SHH campaign, such as residents' houses, family contributions, and building materials.

Material resources were connected to each other like links in a chain. For example, the availability of residents' houses as an in-kind contribution created an opportunity for the residents to contribute other kinds of material resources such as volunteers and tools. This interconnectedness between specific material resources was essential, particularly in the SHH where the absence of public spaces and lack of communication infrastructure were significant obstacles. In-kind contributions managed to address these shortages and thus played a significant role in facilitating the local campaign.

Similarly, non-monetary materials enhanced the campaign's ability to acquire skills and volunteer labor. For example, by securing the building materials for Al Mufaqara community in the SHH, activists attracted and harnessed the skilled local labor needed to erect brick houses. In-kind contributions mobilized residents and helped them become invested in the end goals of the campaigns, often leading them to provide further material resources to expand the scope of the project—for instance, by increasing the number of houses built through the making of hay-and-clay bricks. Their mobilization and deployment of their material

---

37   Interview with the head of Al Mufaqara, one of the SHH communities, 5 May 2019.

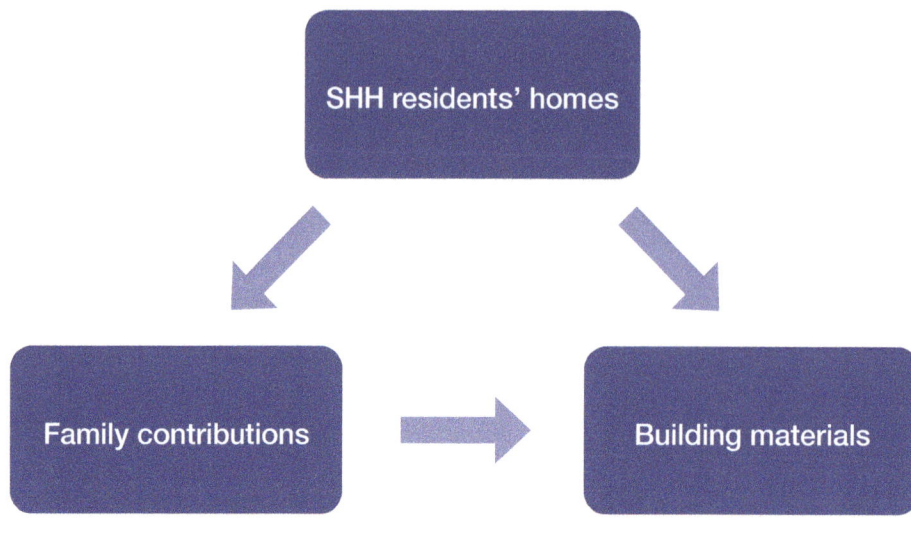

FIGURE 8. Relationships Between Material Resources Acquired by the SHH Campaign and In-Kind Contributions (Homes)

resources was made possible through the non-material resources of the community—including family relations and cultural resources such as *Onah, Ma'dood,* and *Sumud.*

In the JVS campaign, in-kind contributions from JV residents laid the ground for activists to mobilize primary building materials and equipment such as hay-and-clay bricks. These enabled activists to build community centers at the early stages of the campaign in 2003. Later, these community centers were offered as an in-kind contribution enabling women to make food and offer services to visitors, which in turn secured financial support. Moreover, community centers enabled activists to generate non-monetary materials. In return,

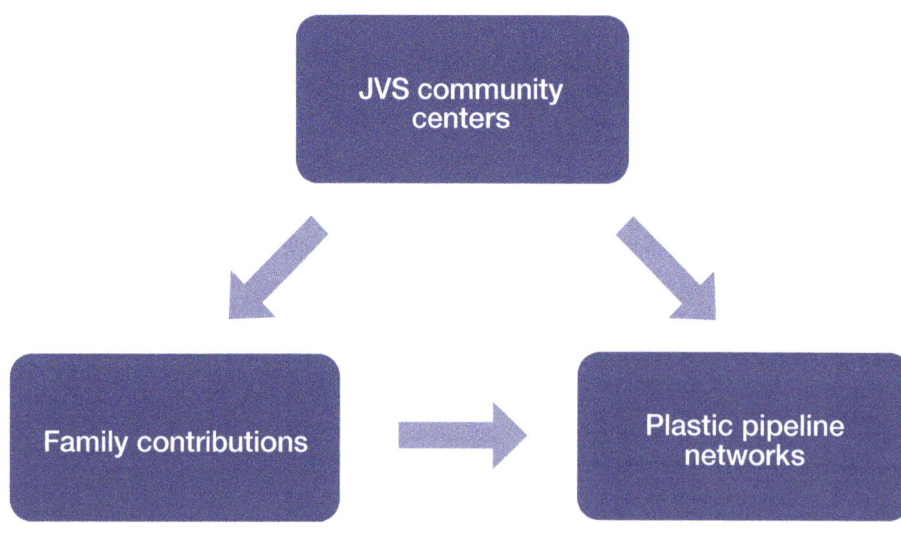

FIGURE 9. Relationships Between Material Resources Acquired by the JVS Campaign and In-Kind Contributions (Community Centers)

non-monetary materials and financial donations encouraged activists to keep planning and working for future actions, which kept activists motivated to offer their homes as meeting spaces. These relationships between different kinds of material resources are illustrated in Figure 9.

In the RV campaign, the PSCC offered its office as a meeting place. Activists were able to use the entire premises both for recruiting volunteers through networking with different PRCs and for securing financial support. Nothing from the PSCC office was used in the campaign's actions, but without the use of the venue it would have been hard for activists to secure tents, transportation for volunteers, and private financial support from small and individual donors. Figure 10 highlights the relationships between the in-kind contributions offered by the PSCC, the financial support provided by Palestinian businesspeople, and the buses used to transport participants to the village building sites. The PSCC office, as an in-kind contribution, enabled meetings to take place where communication and transport could be arranged together with private financial contributions.

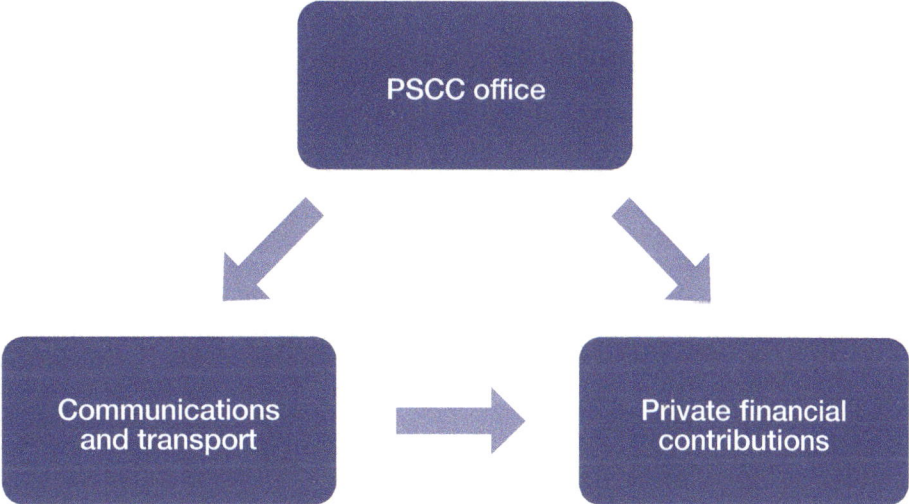

FIGURE 10. The Relationships Between Material Resources Acquired by the Rebuilding Villages Campaign and In-Kind Contributions (PSCC Office)

Means of transportation was one of the most important types of in-kind contribution. Without the transportation provided by local people, nonviolent resistance campaigns would not have been able to reach the levels of participation they did or to bring the infrastructure materials that enabled them to dig and repair roads or install plastic pipeline networks and solar panels. The residents of the SHH and the JV sometimes offered different means of transportation (e.g., donkeys, mules, tractors, and cars) to move laborers and activists, building materials, and other resources to the sites. In all the campaigns, it remained extremely challenging for activists to transfer building materials to the communities. In the SHH, activists used Al Tuwani village as a place where they stored building materials once the Israeli government accepted the village's master plan, allowing the community to build on 3.3 hectares. Materials were first taken there legally. Then, by night, they were transferred to other communities. When donors agreed to provide the SHH and JVS campaigns with building materials, the materials were bought and left in storage places in the nearby cities. No external actors would put their vans at risk to transport the items because of the fear of their seizure and confiscation by the Israeli army and the expense if they needed to reclaim them. Cars, buses, and vans provided by domestic actors were the most important non-monetary material resources in the RV campaign because with them participants were able to reach the work sites.

Human and Organizational Resources
Human and organizational resources made up the third category of material resources that campaign organizers acquired. They included volunteer labor, specific skills, and local organizational networks. This section sheds light on this category of resources, how they were used, and how they helped campaigns acquire additional material resources.

Human Resources
Human and organizational resources include the volunteers and their skills and experiences, as well as the organizational networks already existing in the communities where campaigns took place. These resources were used to obtain support for the campaigns and implement their actions. Volunteers participated in direct actions in the SHH, JVS, and RV campaigns, and their labor was used to help build houses, dig and build roads suitable for cars, install water networks, and build schools and community centers. In other words, human resources were crucial to achieve campaign goals. Skilled lawyers were recruited to follow legal cases associated with the campaigns and to fight for the release of activists from jails and prevent house demolitions. Social resources, such as relationships between families in the SHH or the JV and connections with relatives in other communities aided activists in their recruitment of local volunteers. The availability of specific skills and of volunteers with relevant experience enhanced campaigns' momentum and helped generate building materials. Human resources and the organizational structures of tribe-based, semi-Bedouin societies were harnessed with the help of the campaign organizers, many of whom were from those communities. These semi-Bedouin societies have hierarchies and systems that determine the way communities are organized, and campaign members made use of these structures in their efforts to recruit skilled volunteers.

Volunteer Labor

Volunteer labor was one of the key material resources that grassroots activists mentioned most frequently in interviews and survey responses. The coordinator of the SHH campaign noted:

> *In Areas A and B, companies normally have a contract with the donor to construct a building, but in the SHH the story was different. No company would accept a contract with the providers of the materials. Therefore, local laborers have been the ones who take the responsibility of doing the work. Without local volunteer labor we will never be able to put one stone on another. We are the workers.*[38]

The SHH campaign was mainly focused on building new houses, rebuilding houses demolished by the Israeli army, and renovating or expanding caves for dwelling purposes. These activities relied on the available labor. Most volunteers were sourced domestically: they were residents of the communities or other skilled Palestinian builders who could work quickly, often passing on their skills to younger community members in the process. There were external volunteers too, who were often Israelis and internationals.

The author of this study was involved in the Re-exist campaign in Al Mufaqara—a smaller operation within the umbrella SHH campaign—and was impressed by the commitment of the skilled workers who built houses there. Sometimes they worked for 12 hours a day. The same dedication was seen at Ein Hejle in the RV campaign when the workers renovated houses and rehabilitated the land. Likewise, JV residents showed the same determination when they rebuilt their demolished homes and built schools and community centers.

Yet, there were reasons that made it easier to recruit volunteers in the SHH and JV. First, the goals of these two campaigns aimed to solve the problems of the residents. Second, semi-Bedouin traditions contributed to recruiting volunteers. For example, every evening the community gathered in the house or tent of the family or tribal patriarch, which became a venue where activists could easily disseminate campaign information. Through conversations, they could also decide how to allocate the available skills, experience, and expertise of the family members. Families were encouraged to work with the skilled volunteers and so they too became involved in building their houses or renovating caves and water wells. The commitment they demonstrated was inspired by their own semi-Bedouin customs such as loyalty to the tribe and deference to the authority of the head of the family, The respect that the patriarch enjoys in the community made him an important voice in mobilizing needed resources. In this way, activists in the PRCs were able to benefit from the social and organizational resources available within the communities of the SHH and JV.

---

38   Interview with the coordinator of the SHH campaign, south of the West Bank, 1 May 2019.

Despite the fact that the communities lacked the well-defined rules of local NGOs with their paid staff members and formal structures, they have their own cultural structures that enabled them to be well organized. In addition, there were many local volunteer networks that helped activists find and acquire material resources. Among these networks were local councils, PRNs, and PRCs that enabled activists to connect with domestic and international organizations which, in turn, supported the campaigns with volunteers and building materials, including tents, cement, sand, solar panels, and plastic pipelines.

Building Materials and Equipment

The SHH and JVS campaigns focused on countering the forced displacement of residents, and so the campaigns' main activities involved building houses, restoring caves, and developing infrastructure, including electrical grids and water pipeline networks. Building materials were essential non-monetary resources required for these campaigns to maintain momentum. Activists in the SHH focused on building brick houses and the rehabilitation of caves, while the JVS campaign focused on making hay-and-clay bricks for house construction along with the erection of shelters and tents. In the RV campaign, activists focused on building tents because they are fast to set up and easy to transport. Building materials and equipment were chosen to suit each situation, with a preference for items that are generally available, easy to carry, hide, and transport. Preference was given for tools that are manual and readily available (e.g., pickaxes, hoes, shovels) and also easier to hide and thus avoid the army's attention and confiscation.

Activists chose bricks instead of stones or concrete as their primary building materials because they were cheaper, available in the local market, fast to build with, and did not need plastering before residents occupied their new homes. Activists could build 40 square meters of brick house in little more than two days, as when the Re-exist campaign built 15 houses during the second half of 2012.

The choice of materials can be influenced by both political and practical factors. This study found that activists used tin roofs, partly because they were fast to construct and cheap, but most importantly because the Israelis would not destroy a house on sight if it had a tin roof, while they would immediately demolish a house if it had a concrete roof. According to Israeli law, a tin roof indicates that a house is still under construction, and so an order to stop construction needs to be issued first. If a house has a concrete roof, this means it is finished and the occupying authorities can demolish it. Palestinian activists have successfully exploited this distinction.

Like their counterparts in the SHH, activists in the JV use tin roofs, but they build with homemade, hay-and-clay bricks instead of store-bought bricks for several reasons. Hay-and-clay bricks can be made at home, limiting labor costs to collecting the hay and clay. There is also no need to transport the bricks, which reduces the risk of confiscation by the Israeli army. The hay-and-clay brick is also part of the JV's cultural heritage and suits the area's very hot weather because they are good insulators. In the SHH, caves were rehabilitated because they suited people's lifestyle as semi-Bedouins, another tactic chosen because of the community's heritage. Meanwhile, in the RV campaign, activists built using tents because their strategy has been based on surprise and tents are quick to erect. If activists had built the houses with other materials, the work would have been more time-consuming and would have allowed for discovery by the army.

Materials for constructing houses were not the only building materials activists required. They also needed plastic pipes to build water networks, which became a key resource secured in the SHH and JVS campaigns. Activists used plastic instead of iron pipes because they are cheap and easy to hide, transport, and install. In the SHH, they managed to connect 28 communities with plastic pipe networks. In communities where it was impossible to install water networks, they rehabilitated old water wells and dug new ones.

Electricity networks are another material resource that activists have secured. Electrical grids are not easy to hide, and so PRCs decided to secure renewable solar and wind energy. The infrastructure needed for this is easier to protect from the army than conventional grids because it is harder to confiscate and easier to hide or move when demolition orders are issued, as one SHH activist explained: "We know that the Israeli army is always searching any new infrastructure to come and destroy, thus we built the solar panels on a mobile metal plate with wheels so we can tie them to donkeys and move them when the army comes."[39]

Building materials and equipment were acquired from domestic and external sources with the help of PRCs, PRNs, and international solidarity groups. Internally harnessed building materials came from residents in the form of contributions made directly to the campaigns. Externally acquired resources came from international organizations and were then redistributed to the campaigns through grants.

This chapter showed how activists acquired different kinds of material and non-material resources through donations, individual contributions, grants, and sales. It also explained how campaign actors managed to acquire material resources by relying on socio-cultural resources, especially the traditions of semi-Bedouin communities. The next chapter sheds light on the domestic and external actors who provided the campaigns with the different types of material and non-material resources discussed in this chapter.

---

39   Interview with the head of one of the hamlets in the SHH, 10 June 2019.

Chapter 5. Domestic and External Actors in the Nonviolent Campaigns

This chapter details the different domestic and external actors who have provided material resources to the campaigns or helped activists acquire and harness material and non-material resources (Tables 18, 19, and 20 list the different actors involved in the specific campaigns). Here, we analyze the kinds of actors involved in the campaigns and their connections with different types of material and non-material resources. Their roles are conceptualized and an argument is constructed about the relationships between external actors and material resources and between domestic actors and non-material resources. In the JVS campaign, the residents of the JV and Palestinian actors are treated as domestic actors because they are connected to and affected by the campaign. The Brighton JVS Group and L'Association France Palestine Solidarité (AFPS) are categorized as external actors because they are from outside the OPT and provided financial and non-monetary resources to the JVS campaign.

Table 18. Types of Actors in the SHH Campaign

ACTORS IN THE SHH CAMPAIGN		
DOMESTIC ACTORS		EXTERNAL ACTORS
Palestinian NGOs, PNA, university students, Ministry of Agriculture, Ministry of local governorate	PRC of the SHH, local councils of SHH communities, Al Tuwani Women's Cooperative, SHH residents, PRNs, PSCC	Ta'ayush, ISM, CPT, Comet-ME, ACF, Operation Dove, Action Aid, French Consulate, B'Tselem, Rabbis for Human Rights, Assopace Palestine, Oxfam

Table 19. Types of Actors in the JVS Campaign

ACTORS IN THE JVS CAMPAIGN		
DOMESTIC ACTORS		EXTERNAL ACTORS
Palestinian NGOs, PNA, university students, Ministry of Agriculture, Ministry of local governorate	PRC of the JV, local councils of JV communities, women's cooperatives, residents, PRNs, community centers	Ta'ayush, ISM, CPT, Comet-ME, ACF, Operation Dove, Action Aid, French Consulate, B'Tselem, Rabbis for Human Rights, Assopace Palestine, Oxfam, Brighton JVS Campaign, AFPS

Table 20. Types of Actors in the RV Campaign

ACTORS IN THE RV CAMPAIGN		
DOMESTIC ACTORS		EXTERNAL ACTORS
Palestinian government, Ministry of local governorate, medical relief, Palestinian Red Crescent, office of the prime minister	PRCs, the local councils of Ezerya, Abu Dees and Ez'aiem villages, Stop the Wall and the PSCC, and the monastery of Ein Hejle	Novact, ISM, Anarchists Against the Wall

Domestic Palestinian Actors and Their Role in the Campaigns

In this study, the residents of the OPT, the PRCs, the PRNs, the PNA, and Palestinian NGOs are categorized as domestic actors. All the above-mentioned actors were involved in different degrees with the acquisition or provision of material resources in the studied campaigns. Even though the PNA and Palestinian NGOs helped campaigns secure material resources in the form of monetary and non-monetary resources, the main finding of this monograph is that the crucial role was played by the local residents, PRCs, and PRNs who primarily made in-kind contributions and provided human resources. All these resources were used in interdependent ways. For example, when the PNA provided the campaigns with tents, skilled volunteers from among the communities built them. The following sections elucidate these actors and the kinds of resources they provided to the campaigns.

Community Residents and Their Power to Harness Resources

Community residents were the key domestic actors that provided in-kind contributions, financial donations, and non-material resources in addition to being actively involved in campaign actions. Activists relied on the vibrant social capital of these communities, namely their cultural and social resources, to garner other resources needed for the campaigns. The community residents provided the campaigns with building materials and equipment to dig water wells and renovate caves. They also put their own tractors, donkeys, and mules at the disposal of the campaigns so that materials could be transported to designated sites or hidden to prevent discovery and confiscation by the Israeli army. In-kind contributions by the residents, who offered their homes, food, and drink, further facilitated acquisition of additional building materials from external and domestic actors. Meanwhile, volunteer labor was one of the main material resources that residents provided to the campaigns, with many participating directly in nonviolent actions. Residents also supported the campaigns by sharing non-material resources in the form of local knowledge and expertise in organizing nonviolent actions. For example, their intimate knowledge of the locales helped campaigns overcome the challenges of Israel's monitoring systems. Furthermore, local traditions which encouraged cooperation and hospitality were vital to the campaigns and became an essential non-material resource. The JVS, SHH, and RV campaigns all relied heavily on the non-material resources available to them in the local communities or provided by residents.

The community residents were the first to be affected by the campaigns' outcomes, and so their commitment to and support for campaign goals influenced the viability and momentum of each campaign and their actions. The interviewees from the three campaigns asserted the importance of the material and non-material resources provided by the residents. In the RV campaign, without land from the residents of East Jerusalem's villages, the village of Bab Al Shams would not have been built. Without land from the local monastery and permission

Table 21. A Summary of Material and Non-material Resources Provided by the Residents of the Communities

CAMPAIGN	MATERIAL RESOURCES			
	FINANCIAL	HUMAN AND ORGANIZATIONAL RESOURCES	IN-KIND CONTRIBUTIONS	BUILDING MATERIALS AND EQUIPMENT
South Hebron Hills campaign	Money	• Volunteer labor • Participants in demonstrations • Skills in maintaining infrastructure: water networks, roads, and renewable energy • Skills in renovating caves	• Food, drink, meeting venues, donkeys, tractors	• Sand, bricks, iron, cement • Equipment to dig water wells and renovate caves (bolster, hammers, hoe, hoist, spade, water level, shovel, ladder, masonry, trowel, pickaxe, wheelbarrow)
Jordan Valley Solidarity campaign	Money	• Skilled labor for building community centers, schools, and houses • Skills in maintaining infrastructure: water networks and roads • Skills in agriculture • Skills in making hay-and-clay bricks		• Wood, soil, and hay • Caves (bolster, hammers, hoe, hoist, spade, water level, shovel, ladder, masonry, trowel, pickaxe, wheelbarrow)
Rebuilding Villages campaign	Money	• Volunteers to put up tents • Skills in writing press releases • Skills in communications • Skills in building tents	• Cars, computers, cameras • Use of private land	

from the church, Ein Hejle village would not have remained. Without residents' participation, there would have been no direct collective actions. Support in the form of labor made the process of building houses in the SHH and JV fast and the probability of confiscations lower. Residents provided to all three campaigns non-material and material resources already available within their communities, shown in Table 21.

NON-MATERIAL RESOURCES	
SOCIAL	**CULTURAL**
• Family relations • Neighborhood acquaintances	• Knowledge of the SHH area to facilitate hiding and protecting materials • Legal knowledge • Technical knowledge • *Sumud* • *Onah* • *Ma'dood*
• Neighborhood acquaintances • Family relations • Communal trust	• Knowledge of the JV human and geographic landscape • *Sumud* • *Onah* • *Ma'dood* • Technical knowledge • Legal knowledge
• Friendship • Family relations • Social networks • Relationships with Area C residents	Skills in networking Resistance experience Knowledge of Area C

Domestic Grassroots Actors: The Role of the PRCs in the Campaigns

Chapter 1 defined campaign actors as the domestic actors—from local councils and project committees to PRCs and PRNs—directly involved in campaign actions. Figure 11, on the next page, reflects the relationships between the different campaigns' members. While PRNs form the umbrella for PRCs and provide them with material resources, PRCs are the core entities that are vital for the existence of the PRNs. PRCs are generally not NGOs and are not registered with any Palestinian ministry. They are made up of groups of community-based grassroots activists and can be characterized as participatory organizations. The name of the PRCs—*lejan Sha'beya* in Arabic—was taken from the groups which provided leadership to the nonviolent resistance during the First Intifada.

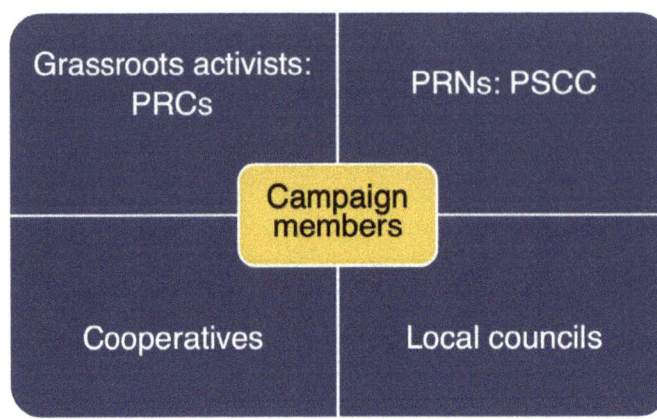

FIGURE 11. The Roles of Campaign Members
in the Nonviolent Campaigns

The PRCs of the SHH and JV committees are formed from the residents of the communities they serve, and so farmers, shepherds, women, and youth are involved. PRC members are responsible for organizing the nonviolent campaign actions. The interviewees for this study noted that there is no bureaucracy at the committee level and that the decision-making process is generally horizontal; however, it sometimes includes a top-down, decision-making approach taken by PRC leaders. In urgent situations that require a rapid response, leaders make decisions without necessarily going back to consult with the other committee members.

The representatives of the SHH and JV communities are responsible for securing and managing material resources. For example, a single activist can represent one community or more depending on their size and circumstances. For example, the PRC for the SHH area consists of seven members who make decisions on the overall goals, direction, and actions of a nonviolent campaign. The smallest local communities, like those in Susya and Al Tuwani, have representation in the PRC subcommittees.

Figure 12 shows the different committees and their connections. During campaign actions, various subcommittees were responsible for organizing their community, mobilizing the residents, and securing material resources from them. For example, if the SHH committee agreed to build a house in Susya village, one of the Susya subcommittees, through its locally based head, would coordinate the action with residents and the SHH committee.

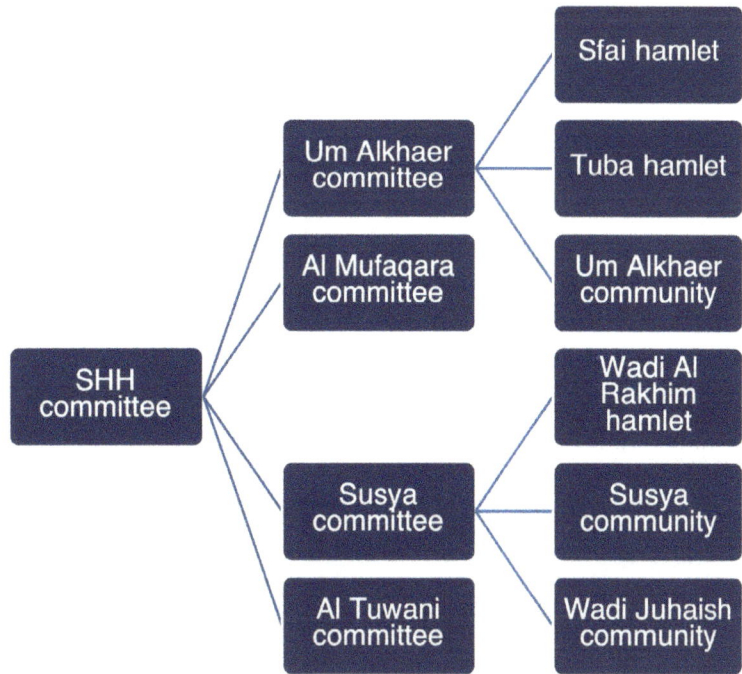

FIGURE 12. SHH Committees and Their Relationships

The SHH's PRC enjoys strong relationships with the local councils, the heads of local families, and the municipality of Yatta (see Figure 13).

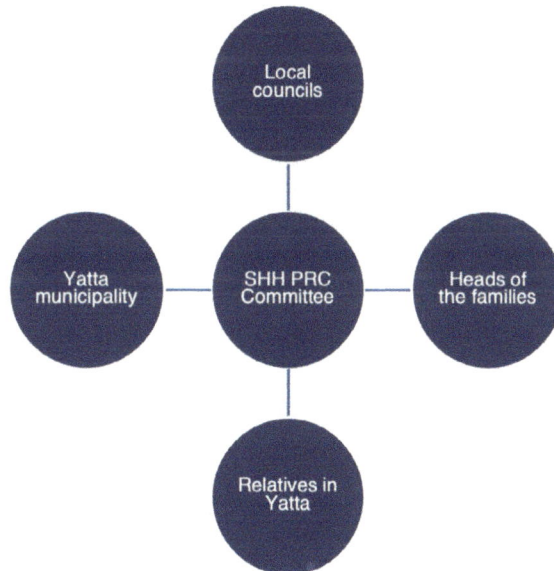

FIGURE 13. Relationships Between the SHH Committee
and Other Local Actors

The SHH committee members have extensive experience in nonviolent resistance. The fact that they are part of the communities they represent has enabled them to garner and utilize material resources.

Table 22 shows the support provided by domestic actors, including state and non-state actors. Non-state actors include NGOs and grassroots actors including PRNs, the PSCC, and Stop the Wall, as well as PRCs and the SHH, JVS, and RV campaigns.

Domestic Grassroots Actors: The Role of the PRNs in the Campaigns

This study focuses primarily on the Popular Struggle Coordinating Committee (PSCC) because of the crucial role it played in providing the three campaigns with material resources and helping them secure and use existing non-material resources. The PSCC members are from communities in Area C. This enabled the PSCC to work closely with those communities and to be directly involved in organizing nonviolent actions.

The PSCC was formed in 2009 by grassroots activists from villages across the OPT that had resisted the segregation wall and the forced displacement of communities in the previous decade. Each PRC—including the SHH and JV committees—is represented by a member on the PSCC's board. The PSCC has operated as an umbrella organization that supports PRCs with material resources, strategic planning, and building activists' capacities. It had to be registered as an NGO to be able to apply for and receive project funding from national and international donors.

The PSCC has an office in Ramallah equipped with internet and communication facilities that was provided as an in-kind contribution to the campaigns' organizers. It also has a general assembly consisting of activists from the PRCs and from which it elects seven board members every two years. The assembly is responsible for organizing nonviolent actions in members' communities, monitoring the board to ensure transparency, and advising the board.

The PSCC adopted a participatory decision-making approach, with decisions made through discussions in the general assembly. The assembly gives the board the legitimacy to make decisions. The PSCC will also consult with others on specific issues. Decisions within the board are by consensus and, when that is not possible, by majority. Its members work as a team, planning together, dividing responsibilities between board members, and following up on decisions and actions together.

Table 22. A Summary of Domestic Actors and the Kinds of Support They Provided to the Campaigns

DOMESTIC ACTORS' SUPPORTING ACTIONS	PRNs, PSCC, STOP THE WALL, PRCs	PNA	LOCAL COUNCILS	NGOs	RESIDENTS OF THE COMMUNITIES
Developed skills and capacity for advocacy and lobbying	✓	✓	✓	✓	✓
Provided lawyers and legal assistance to stop house demolitions	✓		✓	✓	
Distributed cameras to document human rights violations	✓	✓		✓	
Provided volunteer labor	✓				✓
Offered legal support and defended arrested activists	✓	✓			✓
Built capacity and skills to use cameras	✓				
Built locals' legal awareness about their individual rights	✓			✓	
Sourced experienced activists skilled in organizing nonviolent actions and gathered inside houses to prevent demolitions	✓		✓	✓	
Organized training by experienced activists to avoid arrest	✓				
Provided financial support	✓	✓			✓
Offered building materials and equipment	✓	✓	✓	✓	✓
Provided in-kind contributions	✓		✓		✓
Arranged tours to the resistance sites that helped activists network with the PNA, NGOs, and INGOs	✓				✓

The SHH and the JV are priority areas for the PSCC. The organization has offered communities various material resources such as money, building materials, flags, banners, and printing materials, and it has also facilitated networking with other Palestinian and international actors.

The PSCC's members are known as expert activists who have used their existing experience and knowledge of community-based, non-material resources to mobilize locals to support and to join specific campaigns. The PSCC has conducted many workshops and training sessions in nonviolent methods to develop the strategic and tactical capacities of campaigns and to help them maintain momentum, as one PSCC coordinator noted: "Since 2009, we organized different workshops for the residents of the SHH and the JV about the process of legal defense. We also conducted video training and nonviolent training for activists."[40] These actions strengthened the campaigns in the SHH and the JV and facilitated networking between different PRCs as well as mobilizing material resources from domestic and external actors.

The PSCC has built projects with several international, Israeli, and national partners to maintain resources for the provision of legal defense. For example, the PSCC signed a contract with Gaby Laski's legal office in Tel Aviv so that their team of Israeli human rights lawyers could partner with the PSCC in defending Area C activists. It has also made fundraising calls to international solidarity groups to cover the cost of posting bail and other fines for arrested activists.

The PSCC organizes nonviolent campaigns in different areas in the OPT—including the RV campaign—and has supplied volunteers to help with campaigns and money to buy building materials. For example, the PSCC has provided building materials to the Al Mufaqara community in the SHH. It has supported the people's struggle to keep living on their land and has offered help when the community has been endangered by illegal settlements. The PSCC has also covered costs for printing materials, computers, and cameras, and it has paid fines and bail for arrested SHH activists. In addition, it has provided the community with enough building materials and volunteers to construct 15 brick houses. These houses have symbolically and practically resisted Israeli policies of forced displacement, emphasizing the permanent nature of the community's presence in the area. The PSCC has also supplied the SHH committee with t-shirts carrying the SHH logo for summer camps, among other small but important gestures. Furthermore, they have supported the JVS campaign with legal training and with funds to cover the costs of hiring lawyers.

The Palestinian National Authority and Its Role in the Campaigns
Despite the fact that Area C is not under the PNA's sovereignty, as well as the lack of trust in the PNA and the sense of frustration felt by many Area C residents, the PNA has provided

---

40   Interview with the coordinator of the PSCC network, Ramallah, 16 June 2019.

local campaigns with some monetary and non-monetary resources. These resources were used to cover the costs of conducting campaign actions, legal efforts, and infrastructure projects in the SHH and the JV. For example, in the SHH campaign, the PNA provided financial support to build roads, water pipeline networks, schools, and clinics. The president's office donated $38,000 in financial support for the building of Al Tuwani school in the mid-1990s. The PNA also supported legal defense work by providing lawyers and covering court fees to support activists who had been charged by the Israeli occupation forces. This support was provided through the Legal Defense Committee, an office of the PNA. Additionally, the prime minister's office provided the PSCC with $13,000 monthly payments for about four years from 2010 through 2013.

The Palestinian NGOs and Their Role in the Campaigns

The survey and interviews conducted for this study illustrate that a wide range of Palestinian NGOs have provided the SHH and JV with material resources, mainly in the form of building materials and equipment. Among these organizations are the Applied Research Institute Jerusalem (ARIJ), the Ma'an Development Center, the Palestinian Agriculture Relief Committees, and the Palestinian Medical Relief Society. The building materials these Palestinian organizations provided to the campaigns were generated indirectly through grants from international organizations and the Palestinian government. The NGOs redistributed these materials to the campaigns via the local councils and the project committees. The focus of ARIJ and the Palestinian Agriculture Relief Committees was on providing the SHH and the JV with agricultural materials. For example, they gave both campaigns plastic water pipelines and the JV residents greenhouses and solar panels. Meanwhile, the Ma'an Development Center provided infrastructure materials.

External Actors and Material Resources

The committees and networks leading nonviolent campaigns have managed to secure a wide variety of material resources from a range of domestic and external actors. Table 23 illustrates the types of external and domestic actors who provided various resources. The external actors were state actors such as EU representatives and the consulates in the OPT. Other external actors included the non-state solidarity and aid organizations whose involvement was shaped by the kinds of repression communities were experiencing and the types of nonviolent actions they pursued. Additionally, lack of infrastructure attracted support from these aid organizations, while human rights violations led to PRCs and PRNs networking with human rights organizations and solidarity groups. The following section categorizes the external actors who have provided or helped Palestinian nonviolent campaigns with different types of material resources.

91

Table 23. Categories of Actors in the Nonviolent Campaigns

TYPE OF ACTOR CATEGORY OF ACTOR	DOMESTIC ACTORS	EXTERNAL ACTORS
NONVIOLENT CAMPAIGN ACTORS	Grassroots activists: • Residents, PRCs, PSCC • Local councils, project committees	Solidarity groups
STATE ACTORS	PNA	Foreign state actors, the EU and its representatives, state consulates
NON-STATE ACTORS	NGOs	INGOs

Foreign Governmental Actors

External governmental actors represented the foreign states that provided the campaigns with material resources. Some of these government actors provided the campaigns with material resources directly while others supported them with material resources indirectly via INGOs or NGOs. For example, the French consulate has directly provided the SHH campaign with building materials and solar panels, and it has also offered tents to the residents of Al-Mkhoul village. Where and when the campaigns lacked material resources, they reached out to—and were often successful in securing some part of these resources from—other governments or nonprofit organizations they partly funded. It is worth noting that state agencies intervened with tents when the Israeli occupation forces demolished families' houses in both the JV and the SHH. Several state agencies, including the British and French consulates and the Spanish Agency for International Development Cooperation, also provided the campaigns with material resources.

Israeli Peace Groups and Israeli Human Rights Organizations

The opponent's society can play a crucial role in helping a campaign that challenges its own government. This phenomenon can be examined in the wider context whereby the oppressor's society can generate material resources for the oppressed people's campaigns in cases of foreign occupation. The activists interviewed for this study have acknowledged the strategic role of Israeli organizations in helping them network with international actors on behalf of communities in the SHH and the JV. Many Israeli organizations have provided these communities with a wide range of material resources, as the examples here illustrate.

B'Tselem, an Israeli human rights organization, provided SHH volunteers with cameras and laptops. They also supported activists with non-material resources. For example, they trained activists to use cameras to document human rights violations. They also provided lawyers to help people under arrest and open legal cases for those attacked by Israeli settlers. B'Tselem played a crucial role in helping campaigns acquire material resources from external sources by advocating for the JVS and SHH campaigns with Jewish communities such as Jewish Voice for Peace and international organizations such as the EU missions.

Comet-ME is an Israeli-Palestinian organization founded in 2008 in the SHH. It has provided SHH communities with solar panels, wind turbines, and water tanks. The organization has managed to reach every single family in the SHH and provide them with renewable energy. Comet-ME has recently targeted the JV and has started to install solar panels for communities there. It trained two people in each SHH community to maintain and fix any problems with these renewable energy systems.

Rabbis for Human Rights drew the attention of Israeli and international societies to the Israeli army's violations of rights in the SHH and the JV. The organization also provided the SHH campaign with volunteers and covered the court fees for legal cases. It paid the court fees of Susya village in the SHH's case in Israel's Supreme Court.

Ta'ayush is an Israeli-Palestinian organization that has provided volunteers to local Palestinian campaigns to assist in rebuilding houses. Its volunteers usually help farmers with cultivating their land and protecting them from settlers' attacks. It has also offered protection to shepherds. Its volunteers have advocated for the SHH and helped the campaign network with a number of international actors who subsequently provided their communities with material resources. Ta'ayush has had a permanent presence in the SHH since 2002. Its intervention in the JVS campaign is recent and limited compared to its work in the SHH. The organization played no role in the RV campaign.

International Organizations

This study finds that international organizations have played an active role in providing material resources for Palestinian communities in Area C. Some of these organizations, identified below, are focused on aid while others are focused on solidarity.

Action Against Hunger is one of the international organizations that has supplied the communities with tents for families whose homes have been demolished by the Israeli army.

Assopace Palestina (AP) is a network of local groups in Italy united in their commitment to promoting peace and justice. This network emerged in 2012 across Italian cities and is engaged in a range of campaigning, lobbying, and other advocacy activities. Campaigns include support for the Open Shuhada Street movement and work to mobilize concern around Palestinian prisoners, the spread of settlements, and the suspension of the 2000 EU–Israel Association Agreement. AP has been solid in its support of popular struggle in Palestine and has organized visits to the OPT and speaking tours of Italy by Palestinian activists. AP's funding has been secured through subscriptions, public collections, and private donations.

Novact (International Institute for Nonviolent Action) is a Spanish INGO committed to nonviolent conflict transformation. It has implemented projects in Palestine for which it obtains funding from the European Union and donations from Spanish private and municipal sources. Novact has run several programs in partnership with the PSCC, including sponsoring an MA program with Al Quds University. It has enhanced legal protections for human rights defenders in the OPT. Another dimension of its work is research and advocacy, which is evident in the campaigns it has run in Catalonia and Spain to expose the arms deals and security relations that link Israel and Spain.

Operation Dove is an activist organization, based in Italy, which was founded in 1992 during the war in Yugoslavia. Since 1995, Operation Dove volunteers have stayed in conflict zones, living permanently with the residents of these communities. Operation Dove volunteers have had an active presence in the OPT since 2004. They usually accompany SHH villagers and monitor and document human rights abuses by Israeli settlers and soldiers. They have offered young people training to help them use cameras and write reports to document human rights violations. Operation Dove accompanies farmers to help them reach their land and documents the Israeli attacks against them, which helps to undermine the power of the occupation. Its volunteers document the Israeli army's actions and the nonviolent discipline of the farmers. When the army's soldiers see their cameras, they refrain from acts of provocation. This kind of solidarity from international activists is vital in increasing the resilience of Palestinian people. Operation Dove also spreads the Palestinian message in European countries and this has attracted the involvement of other actors who have provided the SHH campaign with material resources. They covered travel costs for some activists so that they could disseminate their stories of life under occupation.

Oxfam was one of the first external actors to supply communities with building materials. Interviewees acknowledged the great impact of these material resources on the SHH campaign, especially the materials that immediately followed the eviction of the 15 communities in November 1999.

Categories of International Actors and Their Support

Table 24, on page 96, provides details regarding the support offered by external, international, non-state actors in the SHH campaign. This study has found that there are three categories of international organizations that support communities in Area C.

The first category comprises aid organizations with branches in Palestine which have worked with the SHH project committees, local councils, and the JV committees. These organizations have provided the SHH and JV committees with building materials and equipment, mainly in the form of tents, tools to renew water wells, and mobile toilets. Sometimes they have provided communities with livestock feed, such as barley. Interviewees appreciated the material resources provided by these organizations as they built their resilience and steadfast commitment to stay on their land, especially following the demolition of houses and shelters. The work of these organizations lacked bureaucracy, allowing activists to quickly use the materials from aid organizations to transform their communities from a reactive to a proactive posture.

The second category of organizations that have provided assistance includes the civil society organizations and networks that supported PRCs and PRNs with non-material resources such as training on capacity-building, advocacy, protection, and networking. In one example, the PSCC contracted an experienced Palestinian journalist to give training to campaign members with the help of another journalist from KURVE Wustrow (an organization based in Germany). Training of this sort happened with the help of INGOs, and they sometimes covered the expenses of training sessions through grants acquired from state agencies. INGOs also supported advocacy and lobbying. When activists documented house demolitions and acts of direct violence perpetrated by Israeli occupation forces, international solidarity groups and INGOs trained them to publish materials online and disseminate them effectively. They also covered training fees to build activists' skills in filmmaking. On some occasions, Assopace and ISM covered travel expenses for activists to go on tours in the EU to advocate for their rights. Assopace brings two residents from the SHH to Europe annually and covers their expenses so that they can advocate for their campaigns which, in turn, generates financial support for the campaigns.

The third category of supportive bodies consists of the external solidarity groups and organizations that supported the PRCs and the PRNs with financial assistance, protection, advocacy, and acts of solidarity on the ground. The interviewees emphasized that these associations offer the most useful support for nonviolent campaigns because their financial assistance is unconditional and not tied to the performance of a certain activity or the completion of a specific project. Money was given to the PRCs to be used for any nonviolent action that the activists determined to be useful on their own terms. Some of the international organizations that provided this support were working directly with the communities while others were working through the PSCC.

Solidarity groups such as ISM and Operation Dove helped activists build their skills through teaching them English and Italian language skills. This kind of skills-building was possible because these groups have a constant presence in the communities. For example, there is a group of youth in the SHH who can speak good Italian because of their close contacts with people from Operation Dove, and they are able to explain their campaigns to them in the Italian language.

Table 25, on page 97, sets out details of the external actors who have been active in the JVS campaign. Few international organizations have provided the RV campaign with material resources as shown in **Table 26**, on page 98.

Table 24. External Actors and Their Actions in Support of the South Hebron Hills Campaign

EXTERNAL ACTORS' SUPPORTING ACTIONS	SCI	OPERATION DOVE	NOVACT	KURVE WUSTROW	AP	OXFAM	ACTION AID	ACTION AGAINST HUNGER	ISM
Shared skills in advocacy and lobbying that helped generate material resources		✓	✓	✓	✓				✓
Offered legal training for expected court battles	✓		✓	✓					✓
Provided cameras and laptops to document human rights violations and campaign actions		✓							✓
Sent skilled international activists to support and join solidarity actions and to protect local activists	✓	✓	✓						✓
Shared skills in documenting and identifying Israeli companies and their activities in the SHH to generate pressure on them to cease their activities			✓						
Gave money to pay for lawyers; legal support	✓		✓						✓
Offered psycho-social support through conducting activities to overcome psycho-social challenges	✓			✓					
Provided capacity-building trainings	✓		✓	✓					
Sent in their staff and representatives to accompany children to schools through monitoring	✓	✓							✓
Offered financial support					✓				✓
Provided building materials and infrastructure equipment						✓	✓	✓	✓
Organized training and shared relevant experience to help activists develop more effective strategies for their nonviolent campaigns				✓					

Table 25. External Actors and Their Actions in Support of the Jordan Valley Solidarity Campaign

EXTERNAL ACTORS' SUPPORTING ACTIONS	SCI	BRIGHTON JORDAN VALLEY SOLIDARITY	NOVACT	AFPS	AP	OXFAM	ACTION AID	ACTION AGAINST HUNGER	ISM
Shared skills in advocacy and lobbying that helped generate material resources		✓	✓	✓	✓				✓
Offered legal training for expected court battles	✓								✓
Gave money to pay for lawyers; legal support	✓		✓	✓					✓
Provided laptops and cameras to document human rights violations and campaign actions		✓							✓
Sent skilled international activists to join and support solidarity actions and to protect local activists	✓	✓	✓						✓
Shared skills in documenting and identifying Israeli companies in the JV to generate pressure to cease their activities			✓						
Provided psycho-social support through conducting activities to overcome psycho-social challenges	✓			✓					
Provided capacity-building trainings	✓		✓	✓					
Sent in their staff and representatives to accompany local activists and monitor the situation	✓	✓							✓
Offered financial support					✓				✓
Provided building materials (wood, tents)						✓	✓	✓	✓
Organized training and shared relevant experience to help activists develop more effective strategies for their nonviolent campaigns				✓					

Table 26. External Actors and Their Actions in Support of the Rebuilding Villages Campaign

EXTERNAL ACTORS' SUPPORT ACTIONS	ANARCHISTS AGAINST THE WALL	ISRAELI LAWYERS	NOVACT	AP	ISM
Helped with media coverage, advocacy, and lobbying			✓	✓	✓
Offered legal assistance in defense of human rights		✓			
Offered legal support		✓			
Provided laptops and cameras to document campaign actions			✓		✓
Sent in their activists to accompany campaigners	✓				✓
Offered financial support	✓		✓	✓	✓

Chapter 6. Leveraging Short-Term and Long-Term Opportunities for Acquiring or Harnessing Resources

Activists in the three campaigns leveraged short- and long-term opportunities to acquire material and non-material resources from domestic and external actors. A summary of key strategies—such as tapping into the urgent needs of communities and linking local struggles with the national Palestinian struggle—were deployed by Palestinian activists to acquire material resources or to tap into the existing non-material resources to secure additional resources, as shown in Table 27. The first column lists the strategies activists adopted and the second column lists the types of resources resulting from these strategies, while the third column provides examples of those resources. This chapter describes each of these strategies in greater detail and illustrates the kinds of resources they generated or harnessed to acquire and secure additional resources.

Table 27. A Summary of Strategies and the Types of Resources Acquired

STRATEGY	TYPES OF RESOURCES THAT THE INITIAL CAMPAIGN STRATEGY HELPED GENERATE (MAINLY MATERIAL RESOURCES) OR TAPPED INTO (MAINLY NON-MATERIAL RESOURCES)	EXAMPLES OF THE RESOURCES GENERATED, HARNESSED, OR USED IN THE CAMPAIGNS
Relying on family relations and family members to promote and share information about the campaign and recruit volunteers	**Material resources:** • Human resources • Building materials and equipment • Financial support • In-kind contributions **Non-material resources:** • Social resources • Cultural resources	• Volunteer labor • Participants in demonstrations • Construction skills • Building tools • Cement, sand • Money • Food, drink, meeting venues • Family relations • Knowledge of local geographical landscape
Tapping into the communities' urgent needs and demands to generate material resources	**Material resources:** • Building materials and equipment • Human and organizational resources **Non-material resources:** • Community acquaintances • Local knowledge	• Bricks, gravel • Solar panels, plastic pipelines • Volunteer labor • Skills in building and renovating water wells and caves • *Ma'dood* • Technical knowledge • Legal knowledge

Table 27, cont'd

STRATEGY	TYPES OF RESOURCES THAT THE INITIAL CAMPAIGN STRATEGY HELPED GENERATE (MAINLY MATERIAL RESOURCES) OR TAPPED INTO (MAINLY NON-MATERIAL RESOURCES)	EXAMPLES OF THE RESOURCES GENERATED, HARNESSED, OR USED IN THE CAMPAIGNS
Linking local campaigns with the Palestinian national struggle to end the occupation	Material resources: • Building materials and equipment • Financial support • Human resources Non-material resources: • Organizational networks • Cultural resources	• Money • Cement, sand, bricks, and iron • Computers, cameras • Skills in maintaining renewable energy • Training • Building networks • The spirit of *Sumud*
Utilizing the opportunity for action created by dramatic events and common threats	Material resources: • Human resources • Building materials and equipment • Financial support • In-kind contributions Non-material resources: • Semi-Bedouin traditions • Neighborhood acquaintances	• Expertise, consultants • Networks with external actors • Media coverage • Building skills • Money • Cement, sand, bricks, and iron
Utilizing customs and traditions to mobilize residents	Material resources: • Building materials and equipment • In-kind contributions Non-material resources: • Cultural resources	• Money • Rooms and offices for meetings • Volunteers • Skills in building houses
Outreach and networking with external actors	Material resources: • Financial support • Building materials and equipment • Grants Non-material resources: • Social resources	• Cement, sand, bricks, and iron • Computers • Office supplies • Government and NGOs' money • Training • Solidarity • Personal relations
Utilizing triumphs of successful legal struggles	Material resources: • Human resources • Building materials and equipment • Financial support Non-material resources: • Cultural resources • Social resources	• Volunteers and participants in demonstrations • Building materials • Money • Skilled lawyers • Networks • Money • Solidarity and awareness • Spirit of *Sumud* • Communal trust
Sharing experiences of "Expert Activists"	Material resources: • Human and organizational resources Non-material resources: • Cultural resources	• Volunteers • Skills and experiences • Money • Resistance experience • Know-how in organizing and campaign planning
Establishing and relying on cohesive relations between PRCs and local councils, and the activists' dual roles and responsibilities as members of both the PRCs and local councils	Material resources: • Human and organizational resources • Building materials and equipment Non-material resources: • Social networks	• Volunteer labor • Plastic water pipelines, solar panels and turbines, building materials • Communal trust • Knowledge of local human and geographical landscape

STRATEGY	TYPES OF RESOURCES THAT THE INITIAL CAMPAIGN STRATEGY HELPED GENERATE (MAINLY MATERIAL RESOURCES) OR TAPPED INTO (MAINLY NON-MATERIAL RESOURCES)	EXAMPLES OF THE RESOURCES GENERATED, HARNESSED, OR USED IN THE CAMPAIGNS
Ensuring media coverage	Material resources: • Building materials and equipment	• Money • Tents • Renewable energy resources • First aid kits
	Non-material resources: • Cultural resources	• Networks with INGOs, NGOs
Promoting transparency about campaigns	Material resources: • Human and organizational resources	• Participants in nonviolent actions • Volunteer labor • Infrastructure material
	Non-material resources: • Cultural resources • Social resources	• Communal trust • Family relations • *Sumud*
Organizing tours for the PNA, NGOs, and INGOs	Material resources: • Human and organizational resources • Building materials and equipment	• Cement, sand, bricks, and iron • Money • Infrastructure materials
	Non-material resources: • Social resources • Cultural resources	• Informal social networks between locals • Communal trust • Formal networks with PNA, INGOs and NGOs • *Sumud*

Relying on Family Relations

This monograph categorizes family relations as a non-material social resource. Campaign organizers relied on family relations in the JV and SHH communities as a strategy to generate material resources. This strategy worked well for several reasons. First, the communities live a semi-nomadic lifestyle, which means that they have strong social relations and internal solidarity. Thus, when activists shared information about the campaign with them, they mobilized family members to become involved in the campaign's actions. Second, the families living in these communities are large and have relatives in other villages and towns. For example, the residents of the SHH have relatives living in Yatta and the residents of the JV have relatives living in Jericho and Tubas. These connections have enabled activists to recruit more volunteers. Third, these families have heads with recognized traditional authority and communal respect. Family structures facilitated efforts to reach family members and, with support coming from the family heads, it made it easier for activists to communicate with and motivate residents to participate.

For these reasons, campaign organizers were able to acquire and harness material resources from the residents of the JVS and SHH communities. Relying on extended family relations and family members generated human resources such as volunteer labor and participants in nonviolent actions. Moreover, the campaigns acquired human and organizational resources such as skills in building houses and non-material resources such as cultural knowledge of how to renovate water wells and caves. Residents drew on their cultural experience and knowledge of living in caves, and they harnessed this memory to renovate those caves destroyed by the Israeli military. They also made other caves effectively habitable for family members. Using social resources like family relations allowed activists to generate material resources and harness existing non-material resources to create new homes.

Tapping into the Communities' Urgent Needs and Demands for Material Resources

Activists strategically designed the goals of the campaigns around solving residents' urgent needs for houses and infrastructure. Communities in the SHH and the JV lacked schools, water pipeline networks, and electricity. These urgent needs offered activists an opportunity to tap into their available domestic resources, especially material resources such as human resources and local labor. It also prompted them to search for other material resources such as solar panels, plastic pipelines, and building materials that would help them launch a campaign to address community demands.

Similar demands stemming from shared deprivations have motivated JV and SHH residents to participate in housebuilding activities and direct collective actions and to offer their individual materials and skills to the campaigns. Tapping into the urgent needs of the communities motivated domestic actors to support the campaigns with material and non-material resources. It also attracted support from external actors in the form of material resources. For example, in the JVS campaign, tapping into the urgent needs of the communities generated infrastructure materials from domestic and external actors. In interviews, the campaign activists stressed that this approach encouraged residents, NGOs, and INGOs to provide material resources for several related reasons. Communities were effectively mobilized when they saw that campaign actions aimed to address their urgent needs. Residents were thus motivated to contribute their skills and time to such campaigns. Also, most of the projects funded through NGOs and INGOs require participation from local communities, and this kind of local participation encouraged donors to provide the needed material resources.

Linking Local Campaigns with the Palestinian National Struggle to End the Occupation

Palestinians living in Area C, like humans everywhere, need houses to live in and services to be available so that they can maintain their lives. The Israeli government has refused to permit Palestinian residents access to services and wants to forcibly displace them. Their refusal is driven by the conflict between the Palestinians and the Israelis over land. Palestinians living in Area C therefore have political motivations for linking their actions against Israeli policies with the Palestinian national struggle to end the Israeli occupation. This nationalization of the campaigns' actions has encouraged the PNA and the political parties to provide them with material resources. The interviewees referred to this process as "positive politicization" and argued that it is good for local campaigns. The presentation of local campaigns as an integral part of the national struggle was a tactic to get the PNA and the political parties involved in providing material resources.

The elevation of housebuilding and infrastructural development to the level of the national struggle generated infrastructure materials such as plastic pipeline networks, building materials, and financial support from the PNA and other Palestinian organizations. This further motivated villagers to volunteer their time and skills to help build houses. Support from Palestinian sources fostered local people's steadfastness in their efforts to stay on the land and defend their existence in the JV and the SHH. Linking the rights of these communities with the national struggle also helped activists harness existing non-material resource, including cultural resources and, particularly, the *Sumud* of Area C residents.

The residents understand that their existence is itself an act of resistance and that non-violent activities offer the most effective ways to protect their land and communities. Some PNA organizations have provided building materials and financial support on this basis. Furthermore, when people are struggling for the right to public infrastructure such as electricity, water, roads, schools, and clinics, they are motivated to participate in collective actions to secure these rights.

Moreover, linking local campaigns with the Palestinian national struggle mobilized the PNA, giving it an opportunity to work toward its own goal to end the occupation through supporting Area C with resources. The PNA's support has the potential to foster residents' trust in the PNA and can also encourage international state actors and solidarity groups to offer more material resources to the campaigns and pressure the Israeli government to respect the rights of the Palestinians in Area C. Campaign actors believe that the PNA increasing its support to residents would inhibit plans by Israel to annex parts of Area C.

Using Opportunities for Action Created by Dramatic Events and Common Threats

Another factor that activists leveraged to secure internal material and non-material resources was a sense of common threat and the dramatic events that are a realization of these threats. This approach was adopted in the SHH in 1999 after the eviction of 15 communities and again in the JV when the Israeli government threatened to annex the valley to Israel. The most recent Israeli unity government announced in July 2020 that it plans to implement the annexation of the JV. These dramatic events were identified by this study's participants as the most important factor in creating a sense of common threat. They used this threat to mobilize residents of the SHH and the JV—as well as national and international actors—to intervene on behalf of the campaigns. An activist woman from the SHH explained:

> *After November 1999, there was nothing more to lose except our land, so it was a matter of "to be or not to be." It was the time when we managed to form a PRC which depends on the activists from the SHH. We started to organize activities and networking with the Israeli and international activists.*[41]

These dramatic evictions attracted Palestinian and Israeli media attention, even though there were no telecommunications within the affected areas. The media coverage of the evictions motivated Israeli associations and Palestinian organizations to provide material and non-material resources. The coordinator of the SHH campaign explains that "The first [organizations] who came to our villages were B'Tselem, Peace Now, and Rabbis for Human Rights. Also, from the Palestinian side there was the National Defense Committee."[42] The National Defense Committee was created in 1996 to provide legal support to Palestinians living in Area C. In 2005, it was incorporated into the Palestinian government as a ministry to financially support Area C residents in their legal struggle in the Israeli courts. These Israeli and Palestinian organizations have mobilized many other organizations. For example, in 2001, Oxfam provided building materials for water wells and toilets for most families. Residents of the SHH acknowledged the importance of these resources at the time and were able to identify that they increased the resilience of the affected communities.

Dramatic events also enabled campaign organizers to harness non-material resources such as semi-Bedouin traditions and neighborhood acquaintances, which in turn generated in-kind contributions and financial support.

Utilizing Customs and Traditions to Mobilize Residents

The campaigns targeted semi-Bedouin communities, which are well-known for their customs and traditions, including their strong sense of belonging to the land. Activists' strategies for harnessing material and non-material resources depended on using customs and traditions to mobilize residents. For example, when activists wanted observers to monitor the Israeli army's movements so they could effectively transport material resources, they relied on the tradition that the residents are shepherds and are on the hills all day grazing their sheep

---

41   Interview with the head of the Al Tuwani cooperative, one of the active members of the SHH committee, 17 June 2019.

42   Interview with the coordinator of the SHH campaign, south of the West Bank, 1 May 2019.

where observation is part of their daily work. They also used customs such as strong family relations among semi-Bedouins to mobilize volunteers to build houses. One tradition of which activists made particular use was the willingness to help and support others. For example, this was used in the RV campaign in Ein Hejle, a site close to the Bedouins. A group of Bedouins volunteered every night to send food and drink to activists, which they carried out as part of their tradition of supporting their neighbors and their ethos based on generosity, resilience, and belonging.

Outreach and Networking with Domestic and External Actors

The PRCs have relied on their cohesive relationships, cooperation, and networks with local councils, project committees, and PRNs to generate internal and external material and non-material resources. These have arisen in response to the needs of the SHH and JV communities, the external threats from the Israeli occupation, and the communities' dual membership in local councils and PRCs. Dual membership was conducive to strong collaboration between these organizations and aided campaigns in their determination of priorities and strategies for the acquisition of material resources. Furthermore, cooperation between PRCs and local councils secured labor for infrastructure projects, with the councils securing building materials and the PRCs recruiting volunteers. As the mayor of Al Tuwani explained:

> In 2009, the PNA through the Ministry of Energy provided us with the power grids. The good relationship and the integrative role between the council and the PRC strengthened our position and convinced the Ministry of Energy to provide us with the materials. Our demands were based on increasing the resilience of the SHH's people and preventing the eviction of the residents in these rural communities.[43]

As noted earlier, PRCs have lacked the infrastructure that would allow them to communicate effectively with each other, with their volunteers, and with the international community. To tackle this problem, after 1999, grassroots activists held meetings with Palestinian NGOs and related Palestinian ministries at which they requested material resources and support to help them communicate with international allies and agencies. Their ability to secure material resources from Palestinians was also constrained by communication and transportation limitations. Therefore, they organized actions that relied on the limited resources they could source from locals and then mobilized people from outside their communities through phone calls and meetings. They also built relationships with local journalists to gain coverage of Israeli violations of residents' rights, such as house demolitions and evictions. Some Palestinian

---

43   Interview with the mayor of Al Tuwani village, south of the West Bank, 20 May 2019.

organizations translated their news into English, and this enabled them to get the attention of national organizations and enhance national and international solidarity.

Face-to-face meetings between local activists and international solidarity groups helped international actors gain a deep understanding of the situation people faced in the SHH and the JV, enabling international actors to offer specific material resources in response. As one of the SHH's volunteer laborers explained:

> *When we go to plant trees, we coordinate with the farmers who own the land and the people of the village. We coordinate in advance with the Israeli activists, and they bring the olive trees. At the end of the activity, we agreed on the time and place of the next activity because there was no internet or even communication. We organize regular meetings between the activists and the committee members, and it became a pattern.*[44]

In the JV, when volunteers from the AFPS stayed with Palestinian activists for a few months, they carried out a needs assessment to identify the materials that would help the campaign. The group members decided, in consultation with the local activists, to run a campaign in France to fund a bus so that they could transport activists to campaign events and bring students to schools. Within one year, the AFPS had raised €24,000 to buy the bus. When SHH and JV activists networked with international solidarity groups interested in supporting their campaigns, group members returned to their home countries and informed and motivated others there to raise funds for the campaigns. The material resources provided by solidarity groups are the only resources which can be used freely by activists without any restrictions; material resources provided by aid organizations or state agencies are always regulated.

As has already been noted, local campaigns have benefited from a snowball effect which has seen Israeli activists play a crucial role in building productive relationships between grassroots activists and international organizations. This has enabled activists to work with international solidarity partners and develop plans for how to strengthen campaign activities. When local and international activists worked closely together in conducting needs assessments, they identified material resources necessary for the campaigns. This ensured that once local PRCs received these resources they were useful and suited local needs. Resources donated without such close relationships would not always fit the needs of a campaign. Visits were also beneficial because, after international activists left, they continued to advocate for the rights of Area C and encouraged others to support or join the campaign.

In the SHH campaign, grassroots activists held meetings with a range of Palestinian organizations and officials, including the Ministry of Local Government, the Ministry of

---

44   Interview with a volunteer laborer from the SHH, 19 June 2019.

Agriculture, and the Palestinian National Defense Organization—which later became the ministry responsible for the annexation wall issues. Notably, these meetings were held in the organizations' offices located in big towns, and so the local activists bore the burden of traveling when they lacked means of transportation.

To combat this problem, grassroots activists invited these officials to visit their communities and organized tours for the PNA and the NGOs. These visits fostered networking and mutual understanding and helped generate new material resources from Palestinian state and non-state actors. During their meetings with officials—and in a bid to generate greater publicity—activists urged people to support their actions using local Arabic media, especially when critical events such as demolitions or violent attacks were taking place.

Grassroots activists have also used their personal relationships with decision-makers in the PNA to generate material resources. For example, from 2010 to 2013, they had regular meetings with then–Prime Minister Salam Fayyad who was responsible for giving the PSCC $13,000 monthly to cover the expenses related to nonviolent activities in Area C.

By connecting their local struggles with the Palestinian national struggle, activists have been able to convince powerful Palestinian actors to support them with various material resources. The prime minister connected activists with the ministries best able to provide relevant competencies and material resources, leading to what one activist called the "positive involvement" of Palestinian actors. The grassroots activists adopted the tactic of involving Palestinian actors in their planning so that they were aware of the importance of the actions taking place, as one activist explained: "We never approached the PNA asking them for material resources after a nonviolent campaign happened. We always asked them in advance, and after discussing with them the importance of the campaign and how it will help in solving people's problems."[45] In other words, grassroots activists were involved in joint planning with the PNA's representatives, convincing them that these nonviolent campaigns could be seen as part of the national struggle for Palestinian independence.

Long discussions and meetings between activists and the residents of the JV and SHH communities have fostered cohesive relations and motivated people to provide material resources. One of the activists noted that "when we met and discussed the activities, we were able to share responsibilities and divide the tasks among us. This helped us determine the kind of material resources needed and who would provide them."[46] The early steps taken in both the JVS and SHH campaigns involved PRCs working with community residents and advocating on their behalf against violations of their rights. If PRCs do not conduct this kind

---

45   Interview with one of the co-founders of one of the PRNs, center of the West Bank, May 17, 2019.

46   Interview with an activist from the north of the JV, 18 June 2019.

of work at the local level, residents will not provide their time, skills, and money to the campaigns.

Utilizing Triumphs of Successful Legal Struggles

Small legal triumphs motivated the SHH, JVS, and RV campaigns to be more proactive. These victories were a morale boost that prompted greater numbers of participants in the campaigns and that gave them access to more material resources, including infrastructure equipment. The SHH campaign coordinator explains how important the legal struggle was in mobilizing resources after the Israelis had evicted the 15 communities:

> *We focused at the beginning on the legal process. With the help of Israeli and Palestinian lawyers, we managed to raise an appeal against the eviction to the Israeli Supreme Court and we had the decision after three months that the people have the right to come back to their villages. From that time, people came back, and they continued their resistance.[47]*

The legal struggle produced a tangible result that was vital in stimulating further action, as another activist stressed:

> *If we succeeded to return to our villages, then we can claim the land settlers took in the past. After consulting the lawyers, we opened legal cases to claim the land back. Before the return of the people to their villages, there was a barrier of fear, but, when we started to go back to the land and organized ourselves, we overcame that barrier of fear. This has been used as a tactic to recruit participants in the nonviolent actions.[48]*

In the RV campaign, the legal steps activists took to postpone the eviction of activists in Bab Al Shams and Ein Hejle increased participation, and, in fact, hundreds of Palestinians joined the actions. In the SHH and the JV, the PRC launched several legal cases against house demolitions and the firing zones, which postponed the demolition of their houses. The Israeli army officers were trying to negotiate directly with the locals, using a "carrot and stick" policy to weaken the residents' legal positions. But after the residents became aware of their rights, they blocked these direct channels of negotiation and sustained the legal struggle.

The Israeli policies in Area C were implemented gradually, and because they deliberately targeted small groups they did not prompt open, collective actions. However, there was a massive and sudden change after November 1999 as the SHH residents were motivated to use legal struggle and collective nonviolent actions. This led to media attention and was

---

47   Interview with the coordinator of the SHH campaign, south of the West Bank, 1 May 2019.

48   Interview with the head of Al Mufaqara, one of the SHH communities, 5 May 2019.

ultimately successful as people returned to their villages. Small victories, such as the return of the evicted people in 2000, encouraged people to take part in further acts of popular resistance and claim back the land the settlers took during the earlier phase when more gradual Israeli policies had been implemented. The SHH PRC had further success in the case of Al Tuwani village when they had the village's master plan recognized by the Israeli occupation forces. This increased people's motivation to contribute the material resources needed to build houses and organize collective actions. The tactics of nonviolent resistance employed at Al Tuwani, along with the community's other achievements, have formed a model for other SHH communities.

By connecting their local struggles with the Palestinian national struggle, activists have been able to convince powerful Palestinian actors to support them with various material resources.

In step with their legal defense actions, activists have broken the barrier of fear by working on their land in groups despite the presence of settlers and army repression. As one activist commented, "With the legal struggle, we proved that this is our private land which increased the sacrifice of the people. Then we started going on a weekly basis and even daily."[49] The struggle against the institutional force of the occupation has been conducted through legal channels and has motivated people to continue their personal efforts to resist. The legal struggle was made possible because lawyers and human rights organizations were recruited to pursue cases in the Israeli courts.

The tactic of legal struggle also included defending activists when they got arrested. The Israeli authorities used repression as a major strategy to subdue nonviolent campaigns in the Occupied Palestinian Territories, especially arrests. Over the course of the RV campaign, the Israeli army has arrested more than 120 activists and more than 50 activists in the SHH and JVS campaigns combined in their first two years. Activists and their families have no financial capacity to cover legal fees, fines, or bail. In response, the PRCs have offered legal support to help activists pursue their cases in the Israeli courts. Legal struggle requires financial resources and skilled lawyers who can follow the cases of activists to the point of their release. The PSCC coordinator explained that the organization has spent more than $300,000 on fines, bail, and legal fees in the past decade. This has reduced the time that activists have spent in Israeli jails and has mitigated the punitive repression of the Israeli army. Moreover, this kind of support has encouraged other residents to join the campaign, changing from observers to active participants. It has also fostered internal solidarity among campaign participants.

---

49   Interview with an activist from the SHH campaign, south of the West Bank, 5 May 2019.

Promoting Campaign Transparency

Transparency is one of the strategies which was adopted by campaign organizers to harness and manage material resources from residents and other actors. Transparency involves being open with communities, sharing information with them, and involving them in all stages of a campaign, particularly in the planning and goal-setting stages. In addition to reducing opportunities for criticism and suspicion around decisions, transparency encourages high-quality, collective, and collaborative decision-making processes and reduces the reliance on isolated, charismatic leaders (which has the potential to destabilize campaigns).

In the three campaigns, when activists promoted transparency by including more local people in decision-making, campaigns mobilized even more material resources. Moreover, when residents from the SHH and the JV were involved in decision-making in their local campaigns, and when activists from affected communities played similar roles in the more geographically dispersed RV campaign, civil society organizations were encouraged to offer their support. The availability of these additional resources also helped the campaigns maintain momentum and achieve some of their goals.

Campaign organizers maintained regular face-to-face meetings with PRC members in the villages and discussed with residents how they would secure the resources required for their actions. They also used traditions and family relations to ensure transparency about resource acquisition. This allowed local organizers to secure commitments from the residents, who had themselves supported the campaigns with their skills and experience. This also helped them to come up with insightful ways to implement campaign actions. When residents were involved in this way, they often became volunteers and mobilized the material resources of other residents. Organizers also encouraged information sharing between locals, which contributed to mutual understanding and support.

In the three campaigns, promoting transparency by involving residents in decision-making empowered villagers to take responsibility for accumulating material resources. Wide participation in decision-making processes meant that systems for monitoring the acquisition, use, and management of material resources could be established, encouraging stronger commitments from and trust between campaign organizers and campaign members. It also helped maintain the unity of the campaigns. Promoting transparency by including locals in decision-making processes has enabled PRCs to respond to the demands of communities and has helped them generate material resources.

Organizing Tours for PNA, NGOs, and INGOs

Campaign organizers, with the help of the PRNs and local councils, organized informative site tours for the PNA, NGOs, and INGOs to visit communities in both the SHH and the JV, which proved to be a successful strategy for informing external actors about community needs, campaigns and their goals, and acquiring material resources. The PNA officials' visits to the SHH and the JV started in 2006, and Prime Minister Salam Fayyad visited the communities more than once. The next prime minister, Rami Hamdallah, also visited the two campaigns and provided material resources for infrastructure development, including plastic water pipelines and equipment to improve roads. As a result of these visits, the PNA provided a bus for Al Tuwani's local council to transport children to their schools, and the Ministry of Education helped secure teachers for community schools. Additionally, Salam Fayyad recognized the local council of Susya, enabling the village to benefit from government funds. When Palestinian NGOs visited, they gained a clear picture of the campaigns' needs, and they responded by providing material resources. INGOs also visited the communities and provided funding through grants that equipped the campaigns with material resources. For example, Action Aid established tents as schools in more than 25 communities in the SHH. They also helped with tents and aid materials in the JV.

Activists managed to organize these tours using their relationships with the PRNs. PRC members discussed with each other the idea for each tour, the areas that would be visited, and who they wanted to invite. The residents' demands were communicated by the representatives of the PRCs via the PRNs. For example, the PSCC used its relationships with people in the prime minister's office to arrange a tour and carry the demands of the PRC to the prime minister and his staff. After the tours were organized, local activists then led the tours, taking the opportunity to explain their situation and needs. The PM and the ministers heard their demands and supported some of them. Other demands were not met on account that the PNA does not have authority in Area C according to its agreements with the Israeli government.

Visits from NGOs were normally organized by the PRCs and the local councils. Because they were linked to the implementation of local projects, they could carry out these contacts independently from the PRNs. INGO tours were organized with the PRCs, local councils, and PRNs. For example, the PSCC has a good relationship with Novact, a Spanish NGO. Every time Novact had delegations in the area they contacted the PSCC to arrange a tour to visit the campaign. Also, if residents wanted to update the Spanish consulate or Novact about the situation on the ground, the residents would do so through the PSCC that made arrangements with the locals who did the tours. Consulates and the agencies of each country have financial resources available, and these tours encouraged them to support campaign projects. Sometimes these tours have also generated political pressure on the Israeli government to stop demolitions and recognize villages, as happened in the case of Al Tuwani.

Chapter 7. Managing Material and Non-material Resources

The management of resources is just as important in nonviolent campaigns as is generating those resources in the first place. An ability to secure or harness the right kinds of resources, combined with the effective management or deployment of these resources, can considerably increase a campaign's success. It can lead to greater mobilization and internal unity, and it can help foster greater understanding and trust between residents involved in the campaign and aid providers. In contrast, poor resource management can be a source of division between community members and will impact a campaign negatively.

Material resource management includes the processes of their distribution, deployment, and reallocation. Their effective management involves an accurate assessment of a campaign's needs and requires transparency with the residents about how a resource is acquired and used.

Non-material resource management includes harnessing and deploying often intangible socio-cultural assets to mobilize people. It involves a range of campaign actions that include joint planning with the residents, mapping residents' available skills and knowledge, and ensuring broad involvement of residents who can bring or contribute social and cultural resources.

Chapter 6 analyzed the strategies that campaign organizers adopted to generate material and non-material resources. This chapter focuses on the strategies activists adopted to manage the resources they acquired or harnessed. It also discusses the capacities and abilities that campaign organizers needed to manage resources. **Table 28** summarizes the campaigns' strategies for fostering the effective management processes. In addition to listing strategies developed around specific goals, this table includes specific actions that activists undertook and capacities or capabilities they utilized to ensure the effective management of specific resources. Capabilities here are understood as the knowledge activists have about local norms and traditions and the family structures in a semi-Bedouin society. These capabilities enable them to effectively manage material resources with locals.

Table 28. How Resources and Capacities Were Used Strategically to Achieve Campaign Goals

STRATEGY	GOAL	ACTIONS	CAPACITIES DEPLOYED	RESOURCES GARNERED
• Achieve the maximum number of goals with the minimum number of resources • Maximize the use of limited resources by having clear priorities set and a division of tasks and responsibilities agreed in an operation that functions well	Effective organizational structure	• Dividing responsibilities between activists • Working as a team	• Leadership and meeting facilitation • Networking • Negotiations with locals	• Local activist labor • Trust • Building materials and infrastructure
Deploy constructive resistance to reverse effects of forced removal from the land	Develop infrastructure for housing, transportation, and utilities	• Building roads • Constructing tents and houses • Installing solar panels and water pipelines	• Skills in rehabilitating caves and water wells • First-hand experience in the area • Construction skills	• Elders in the community skilled in rehabilitating caves and wells • Local construction labor
Establish open, transparent, and deliberate processes for making decisions	Avoid divisions and foster democratic and participatory decision-making, fostering unity and transparency	• Involving residents in decision-making processes • Making decisions by consensus among the PRC members	• Leadership and meeting facilitation • Networking • Knowledge of the area, including knowing families and the relationships between them • Relationships with local families	• Buildings for holding meetings • Local activist leadership
Include external and domestic stakeholders in resource management	Effective management of materials and trust-building	• Sharing resource management responsibilities between donors and local activists • Cooperating and networking with broad, loose networks through PRNs and external actors	• Management skills • Logistical skills • Networking skills • The ability to maintain cohesive relationships	• Local activist leadership • Relationships with NGOs, PRCs, PRNs, and local council representatives
Organize in conjunction and in harmony with cultural norms and traditions	• Maintain momentum of a campaign despite lack of organizational networks (e.g., lack of local councils in the SHH campaign) • Maintain the legitimacy of the campaign in the eyes of the locals	• Establish project committees with membership chosen from local families • Harness and utilize the cultural power of Sumud and Onah	• Knowledge of traditions and customs • The ability to maintain relationships between activists and residents, and with heads of families • Communication skills • Skills in cooperating with domestic and external actors • Skills in solving problems and resolution of family disputes	• Local families • Local activist leadership

113

Maximizing Campaign Results with Minimum Resources

The residents of Area C struggled to secure material resources for use in infrastructure activities because of Israeli policies. Activists adopted strategies to manage material resources effectively and reach their goals with the resources they acquired. Their first strategy was to use the minimum material resources needed to achieve the maximum goals. The RV campaign coordinator summarized this strategy when he asked, "Why pay more if we can do it with less?"[50] This strategy involved establishing an effective organizational structure that included clear priorities and agreement on the division of tasks and responsibilities to keep the operation functioning well.

To achieve the largest possible portion of goals, activists relied on their relationships with PRNs, local councils, and the project committee's organizational structure. This structure helped activists effectively manage material resources. The PRCs do not have conventional organizational structures designed to acquire material resources systematically and allocate them to a variety of individuals, groups, and campaigns. The PRCs' and the PRNs' actions—such as working in teams and in cooperation with the local councils, project committees, and the heads of families—enabled activists to manage material resources effectively. For example, in the Al Mufaqara campaign in the SHH, activists reached an agreement with the residents that the brick houses would be simple dwellings of 40 square meters each, and the ceilings would be made not from concrete but from tin. They also agreed to use the residents' building skills to construct the houses. This management approach created clear priorities, divided responsibilities, and enabled them to build 15 brick houses.

Activists' abilities to negotiate with the residents and their coordination with the local councils and the project committees allowed the campaign to use the smallest possible amount of material resources to build more houses and carry out other infrastructure activities. For example, two years after building the houses in Al Mufaqara, Comet-ME and the PSCC provided the community with solar panels. Efficient management and the use of clear priorities helped activists create more homes, establish infrastructure, and organize additional nonviolent actions. It also eased the pressure that would have arisen if they had to secure all necessary material resources at once.

Working as a team led to the effective management of material and non-material resources. In the JVS campaign, the smallest possible number of teachers ran the schools built from hay-and-clay bricks, which allowed more adult volunteers to work on other aspects of the campaign. In the RV campaign, activists' regular meetings and teamwork enabled them to manage resources effectively and economically. For example, in Bab Al Shams they built

---

50   Interview with one of the coordinators of the RV campaign and co-founder of one of the PRNs, center of the West Bank, 7 May 2019.

large-capacity tents to save money and to cater to more residents. Similarly, they chose the Ein Hejle site because there were already old houses there and so they did not need to bring tents. Strategies like these helped campaigns produce the greatest possible impact from minimal resources.

Establishing Transparent Deliberative Decision-Making Processes

The SHH's nonviolent campaign was launched when there was still no local council to draw on, though a project committee involving the heads of local families did exist. When the PRC was formed, it was based on these families. As the coordinator of the PRC emphasized, "There was no role for the political parties in our community. We represented the families in the communities."[51]

Material resources were managed through cooperation between project committees, local councils, the PRCs, the PRNs via the PSCC, and donors. Cohesive relationships between these actors became crucial, but, as interviewees explained, management issues were also impacted by the kinds of resources managed at any given time. For example, infrastructure projects—schools, roads, water pipelines, and solar panels—tended to be managed by the project committee and external donor. Meanwhile, the PRCs delivered and managed the volunteers who provided labor. The PRCs also led specific advocacy actions, which involved documentation and legal processes in the case of demolition orders or people's rights to public services. Material resources such as banners, speakers, flags, and leaflets needed for nonviolent actions were the responsibility of the PRCs and the PSCC. The latter provided the flags and banners for demonstrations to PRC members who distributed them to participants. After the demonstrations, a member of the PRC collected and stored them for the next actions.

Activists exchanged information about campaigns actions in a deliberative process that enabled them to reach an agreement that informed the decision-making process. This helped them to divide responsibilities between campaign members (including PRCs), project committees, and local councils and helped shape the community's appreciation of the idea that all their projects—even humanitarian ones—could be understood in terms of political struggle. One activist confirmed that "with our presence, we gave the humanitarian projects the form of popular resistance."[52]

The effective management of material resources has depended on including all members of the community in decision-making processes and dividing responsibilities among them. Responsibilities included tasks such as distributing acquired materials to participating

---

51   Interview with an activist from the SHH campaign, south of the West Bank, 20 May 2019.

52   Interview with an activist from the SHH, south of the West Bank, 5 May 2019.

communities or deciding on the quantity and kinds of materials needed to be transported to each site. Sometimes the NGOs, with the PRC and the local council, have even met with individual families to make these decisions collaboratively.

Including External and Domestic Stakeholders in Resource Management

This mixed management style—whereby donors became involved in managing materials with the campaign organizers—was crucial in the early stages of the campaigns because of the absence of local organizations. Mixed management between domestic actors and external donors helped, on the one hand, to ensure that there were enough of the right kinds of materials, and on the other hand, to enable effective local management of materials. Working closely helped build trust between locals and donors, as the head of one community explained: "When Oxfam implemented their project in the SHH communities, they visited each family with the project committee members and they supported each family with sheep feed, water wells, and toilets."[53] At this point, there was no organizational network functioning in the community, and the hands-on engagement of donors with residents fostered transparency and inclusiveness which, in turn, helped residents mobilize for nonviolent actions. Working together enabled activists to build their capacities in managing material resources, skills they learned from external donors. Moreover, they built networks with external actors who ultimately supported the campaigns.

Coordinating with Project Committees and Local Councils

In the three campaigns, resource management was affected by the organizational structure of the committees involved. The PNA only organizes and recognizes local councils for communities where there are more than 500 inhabitants, and there were no SHH communities of that size. Instead, the residents set up project committees, which were recognized by the PNA. They had a lower status than a local council, and their membership consisted of local families in line with the traditions of Bedouin communities. Over decades, it became a cultural norm that each family must be represented in the committee and the head of the committee must be from the largest family.

These project committees were responsible for offering infrastructure services such as water, electricity, and roads to SHH residents. They had no long-term development plan to expand their infrastructure services to new areas, but they did have short-term plans to provide services to the residents. After 2007, only Al Tuwani had a local council that was recognized by the PNA. Later, in 2013, the PNA formally recognized a local council for Susya village

---

53   Interview with an activist from the SHH, south of the West Bank, 10 June 2019.

even though they had fewer than 500 inhabitants, because there was an urgent need for a representative organization that would be able to secure material resources through grants from the PNA.

Since 2007, the seven-member Al Tuwani council has had a building in which the community could meet. In 2015, the PNA established a joint service council for all SHH communities. Following the PNA's recognition of the Al Tuwani local council as the official body tasked with administrative functions—which resulted in their being able to receive materials and financial support from the PNA to run public services—the council acquired material resources from Palestinian actors and submitted regular financial reports approved by the PNA.

The project committees, and later the local councils—both affiliated with the PNA's Ministry of Local Government—established an organizational structure that helped manage material resources. Although they received very few material resources for their infrastructure projects from the PNA, they managed to generate them directly from SHH residents.

Several factors have helped the local councils to manage these material resources. Many council members are also members of the PRC. This fostered cohesive relationships between the project committees and the PRC and, later, between the local councils and the PRC. The social intimacy between activists in the SHH, as well as their semi-Bedouin traditions, advanced their loyalty to their communities and meant that they were recognized and welcomed by their people. This enhanced their unity and transparency with each other, which has helped them manage material resources effectively. Their shared purpose has also helped them generate and manage material resources effectively, and the crossover between local councils and PRC members has allowed for integrated strategies to be developed for their management and use.

Organizing in Harmony with Cultural Norms and Traditions

Material resources harnessed from residents were managed in conjunction and in harmony with cultural norms and traditions. This helped maintain campaign momentum in the early days despite the lack of organizational networks such as local councils and local NGOs. Activists established cohesive project committees drawn from local families and comprised of members with in-depth knowledge of cultural norms and traditions. This enabled the committees to manage resources effectively, for example, by knowing who to talk to in each community about their use and deployment. They also knew the best way to approach community leaders and carry out consultations about how to harness material resources.

As discussed in prior chapters, activists use social capital to generate material resources, but they also use it to manage these resources—particularly those materials acquired from residents themselves. Committee members used the authority of the heads of the communities and the respect they hold to solve problems that arise while implementing campaign actions, as one activist explained:

> When we were establishing a plastic water pipeline between two communities in the JV, one of the locals did not permit them to install it in his land. We went to the head of the community and told him about the problem. The head of the community held a meeting in his home, called all the parties and gave a speech about solidarity, Onah, and Sumud. He emphasized the importance of people's cooperation with the campaign and their neighbors' need for water. At the end of the meeting the man who objected stood up and gave permission to the committee to install the water pipelines through his land.[54]

This is one of many examples showing that traditions and cultural norms can be used to manage resources. If this resident had not cooperated, the committee would have used another, longer path, but this would have meant using more plastic pipelines.

Coordinating with the PRNs in Managing Material and Non-material Resources

Chapter 5 showed that PRNs, including the PSCC, played a crucial role in generating material resources. Their role also included managing material and non-material resources, especially the material resources acquired through grants. Activists coordinated with PRNs to manage these resources because they had employees with the relevant skills needed to produce donor reports.

Most grants were acquired through the PRNs. The PSCC secured funds from INGOs, and then their staff coordinated with the campaign organizers to manage material and non-material resources. For example, the PSCC managed the money and recruited lawyers for a legal project in the JV that was funded by Novact. Similarly, the PSCC managed media and capacity-building training in the SHH as part of a project funded by the EU Commission. Activists coordinated with the residents while the PSCC ensured the effective deployment of the materials and the training. The PSCC also prepared the relevant financial and administrative reports with supporting documents.

Coordinating with PRNs and including them in management processes gave credibility to the campaign organizers in the eyes of the donors, and it ensured the best possible use and deployment of material resources. It also encouraged donors to continue supporting the campaigns with material resources. This was also true regarding financial support from

---

54   Interview with an activist from the north of the JV, 10 June 2019.

solidarity groups, wherein the PRNs hosted the funds in their bank accounts and worked jointly with campaign organizers to manage their use. For example, the Assopace group from Italy would transfer money to the PSCC's bank account to support the JVS and SHH campaigns, and then activists from the campaigns and the PSCC board decided how to use it.

Chapter 8. Protecting Material Resources from Israeli Authorities and the Military

Area C has been under full Israeli military control since 1967 when the Israeli army occupied the West Bank and the Gaza Strip, which means that Palestinians are subject to Israeli military laws. The military permitted the application of the Defense Regulations of 1945, originally issued by the British Mandate authorities to quell growing unrest in Palestine and now used by the Israeli army to deprive Palestinians of their basic civil rights. Military law makes the Israeli army the sole controller of the Palestinians without accountability. In this oppressive context, the acquisition, management, and distribution of resources become acts of resistance in and of themselves. Material resources must be obtained, stored, managed, allocated, and deployed in a clandestine manner. Sometimes resources must be hidden to stave off an Israeli army crackdown and then utilized at the right moment and with a degree of efficiency that maximizes their impact.

In the nonviolent campaigns in Area C, activists have adopted different tactics to overcome Israeli actions that prevent them from building and result in the confiscation of material resources. In all three campaigns, activists strove to secure material resources by tapping into the needs of the communities, networking with external actors, and selling products and services, but they also had to find ways to transport resources to the communities that needed them. Because the army is constantly present in the SHH, it is extremely risky to transport materials to the area. Thus, activists relied on the semi-Bedouin life of the residents and their in-depth knowledge of the area to protect material resources—something especially difficult when settlers are working as the army's agents. As one of the residents recalled, "When we were building a water well, the settlers were observing us, and they immediately informed the army that arrived soon afterward. Yet, we covered and hid the materials or transferred them to another place. When the army arrived, it saw nothing of the real work we were doing."[55]

The challenges faced by activists grew as the Israeli settlers increased their monitoring of Palestinian activities in the SHH after 2006. Settlers are well-equipped to monitor Palestinians' nonviolent activities with equipment such as drones, cars, cameras, computers, and internet resources. In 2006, the settlers established Regavim, an NGO that supports the illegal activities of Israeli settlers in the OPT and is funded by the settlements' councils and international donors. This organization monitors and pursues legal actions in the Israeli courts against any Palestinian construction in the OPT that lacks Israeli permits. An SHH activist from Susya explained how Palestinian activists counter its work:

---

55   Interview with a volunteer laborer from the SHH, 19 June 2019.

We conducted a series of workshops in the SHH to increase the awareness of the residents about Regavim—who are they and their activities in the SHH and other places across the OPT. Also, we taught participants how to discover their activities, identify when they document without permission and when they pretend being an international solidarity group. For example, international solidarity activists introduce themselves to the community while Regavim members do not. They also use drones to document Palestinian activities and file court cases against Palestinians to quicken the pace of house demolitions.[56]

The activists gather information about the members of the organization and distribute this to communities to help them recognize Regavim representatives. Palestinian activists also monitor Regavim's work internationally. It has received funds from international organizations and so activists send the funders reports about Regavim's violations of Palestinian rights.

Despite the constant presence of the army and the help it receives from settlers, residents in the SHH and the JV have used a range of creative tactics to transport materials to campaign sites to avoid their confiscation. In this work, they have relied on their in-depth knowledge of the area and the local lifestyle.

Activists have observers stationed on hilltops to monitor the army's and settlers' movements. Given the lack of mobile communication, activists recruit additional volunteers so they can send signals from point to point until the signal reaches the driver of the tractor who is transporting the materials. These resistance tactics succeeded in the SHH and JVS campaigns because of the lifestyle of the residents. The observers were shepherds and they did not necessarily catch the attention of the army and settlers. As semi-nomads, they are also on the hills daily which ensures relatively uninterrupted observation and up-to-date information for activists about army and settler movements.

If the army catches a driver, soldiers issue a considerable fine and confiscate the materials and sometimes even the tractor. In such situations, the residents of the communities will often quickly gather and surround the soldiers forcing them to abandon their attempts to confiscate the materials and release the driver of the tractor. Normally, a driver is stopped by one army patrol with four soldiers. If activists gather quickly with large numbers before more soldiers arrive, they are often able to prevent the confiscation of the materials. The process of protecting materials also depends on activists' knowledge and experience about the soldiers' tactics and the limits of their authority, including what they can and cannot do without referring to an officer of higher rank. Activists know from experience that they can challenge the army in order to protect materials in some situations, and they also understand that a few soldiers can control a crowd that has no experience and knowledge of the army's regulations.

---

56   Interview with an activist from Susya village in the SHH, 22 June 2019.

One of the activists who had transported materials from Yatta to the SHH recounted this story:

> *One day, I was transporting building materials for Al Mufaqara community. The soldiers stopped me at the entrance of Al Tuwani village. They called the police to arrest me and take the materials. Meanwhile, the Palestinian observers called the people of Al Tuwani village to release me. Women, men, and youth gathered around the army and demonstrated, and I escaped with the materials.*[57]

Another tactic adopted by grassroots activists to avoid the army's confiscations is to disguise their actions to throw off the attention of settlers observing them from a distance. One of the activists explained that "when the settlers or the army come, we move quickly to another place and pretend to be doing other things such as picking up grass from the land while the real work is building a hidden house or digging a water well."[58]

One camouflage tactic involves building a tent and then leaving it for a week. The army does not treat the building of a tent with the same seriousness as it treats house construction—they can ignore the tent, but the house is not easy to disregard. After the tent has been there for a week, SHH activists start building a brick house inside the tent. When the brick house is finished, they remove the tent and put up a tin roof. When the soldiers discover the house, they come and give orders to stop construction. However, by then the work is already done. Yet since the tin roof is denoted under Israeli law as a building still under construction, the army must begin a lengthy legal process before it can demolish it. The residents' knowledge of Israeli military law helped them to work tactically and protect material resources successfully.

The tactic of disguise has also been used to transport materials. For example, when activists transport material resources from the cities and towns they hide them under barley, which is used for livestock feed. Sometimes they wrap up building materials such as cement, sand, and bricks. The people of Al Tuwani managed to build an electric power network by working at night, bringing the electricity poles on the backs of their donkeys from Yatta. They made use of Friday and Saturday evenings when the settlers and soldiers were marking Shabbat, and they also exploited the very limited presence of the army and settlers in the area at times when they would be less likely to be observing the roads.

Locals managed to prevent the confiscation of material resources by the Israeli army by using donkeys. When activists transferred material resources to Bab Al Shams, they sent the tents on the backs of donkeys as a way to hide them from the army.

---

57   Interview with an activist from the Al Mufaqara community, 5 May 2019.

58   Interview with a volunteer laborer, south of the West Bank, 10 June 2019.

Residents of the JV and the SHH have used a wide range of tactics to protect their material resources. For example, they hid food in the Bedouin community to avoid its discovery by the Israeli army. Similarly, in the SHH, activists hid cement in barley bags so that the Israeli soldiers would not discover it. In the JV, activists installed water systems at night to prevent the army from confiscating the plastic pipelines. In addition, they placed grass on the roofs of buildings when they built them so that the army would not discover them when they took aerial and satellite photos.

Using the same kind of night-time tactics, the people of the SHH paved the road that connects Al Tuwani with Alberke village. On a Friday evening, the mayor of a nearby town lent paving machines to the mayor of Al Tuwani so that the community could pave the road overnight during Shabbat. It took them seven hours, and all the people in the SHH volunteered to speed up the work to complete it before dawn. The interviewed residents reported that when they succeeded, they felt empowered and genuinely satisfied with what they had achieved.

The RV campaign involved a large variety of tactics and efforts to avoid surveillance, as the coordinator of Bab Al Shams explains:

Our main concern was how we could transport this large number of people to participate in building the tents and stay in Bab Al Shams village without being discovered by the Israeli army. If we announce the plan, the army will close the road immediately and prevent people from reaching the area. We will also lose an element of surprise that we counted on when a large number of people would suddenly appear in a specific location, because if we go openly to the place the army will not let us reach the place. Thus, surprising them is the only tactic to reach the place. Also, we needed to prepare people well in advance that they will need to stay on site for a long time.

We agreed to announce a winter camp in Jericho to confuse the Israeli army, because if the army know that activists were going to Bab Al Shams they will close the area. One activist took on himself to create an event on Facebook under the heading "Sharing experience and speaking about popular committees" and invited people to attend a week-long winter camp in Jericho. With this, we achieved two goals: first, we opened the way for anyone who wanted to participate and register to join our action; second, we managed to keep it secret without announcing what we were really doing and where. One day after the Facebook event launched, I got a call from a private number. I answered and it was the head of the Israeli civil administration in Jericho, who told me that they heard about our camp in Jericho and they want to know more details. This call relaxed me, because I understood that until now, even if they knew that we were gathering, they still did not know our final plan to reach Bab Al Shams area and not

Jericho as we had announced. But this also meant that they were following us. So, we had to be even more careful.[59]

By using these disguise tactics, activists were able to reach the site and build the tents as envisaged by the campaign. Because activists successfully used tactics of camouflage and misdirection, hey were able to keep material resources available to be used as planned and provided a way of managing them.

Another crucial tactic adopted by activists involved women bothering and distracting the soldiers until the men had finished hiding the materials. In other occasions, women would hide materials while the men distracted the soldiers. A female activist from Al Tuwani sheds some light on women's involvement in hiding campaign resources:

When we started building the village school, the soldiers prevented men from working and threatened them with arrest. We decided that the women would transport building materials during the day and the men during the night. When the soldiers came and asked, "What are you doing?" we replied, "We are bringing water to our houses, not making a bomb."[60]

In the JVS campaign, activists worked at night, especially on Fridays and Saturdays during Shabbat, to complete their tasks secretly and quickly. They worked in the same manner to make bricks at the building sites, and in this way three classrooms were built in JV communities.

A volunteer laborer explained some of the other tactics that were used while they were building the school:

We brought a concrete mixer to do the work faster and we put a tractor next to it and when the army came, we connected the mixer to the tractor to escape and avoided the confiscation of the mixer. We had enough time to prepare due to the observers who gave us the signal when they saw the army approaching.[61]

Through these kinds of actions, Palestinians helped create and change the facts on the ground in Area C. This chapter has highlighted the ways activists managed material resources, whether through the organizational structure of the PRCs and the PRNs or through the tactics they adopted to prevent the confiscation of material resources. Thus, activists secured materials from domestic and external actors and managed them well.

---

59   Interview with the coordinator of Bab Al Shams, center of the West Bank, 7 May 2019.

60   Interview with a woman activist from the SHH, 24 June 2019.

61   Interview with a volunteer laborer, south of the West Bank, 10 June 2019.

Chapter 9. The Impact of Material and Non-material Resources on Nonviolent Campaigns in Area C

Chapter 7 described the mechanisms activists used for managing material and non-material resources, and the previous chapter discussed how activists effectively hid material resources from the Israeli army so that they would not be confiscated. By properly managing their resources—including their clandestine operations to transport building materials to construction sites—activists were able to effectively use these resources to have a positive impact on campaign objectives. This chapter discusses the results of their use of the resources. **Table 29**, on the next page, shows the types of resources deployed in campaigns, examples of each type of resource, the type of provider, and their impact on the campaigns.

Material and non-material resources have had various impacts on nonviolent campaigns in Area C. These impacts were affected by a range of factors related to the kinds of material and non-material resources that were accumulated or harnessed. Other impacts were affected by the organization of the PRCs and the PRNs, which influenced the acquisition and management of those resources. The impact of material and non-material resources has sometimes been affected by the domestic or external provider of a specific resource or by the ways materials were managed by campaign members. Sometimes material resources carried with them the risk of having a campaign lose its autonomy or the danger of external agendas being imposed on activists.[62] Most often, material and non-material resources were seen to produce positive impacts. These resources helped:

1. Increase residents' participation and ability to organize nonviolent collective actions

2. Facilitate and strengthen activists' nonviolent discipline

3. Enable activists to organize actions more frequently

4. Foster transparency, unity, and cohesive relations among residents

5. Mobilize and popularize nonviolent campaigns across occupied areas

6. Sustain nonviolent campaigns for more than ten years, including accelerating building and infrastructure activities, securing financial and transportation means, advancing legal struggle, extending networking and advocacy, deploying effective media communication and documentation actions, and protecting resources.

---

62   The distinct impact of material resources on campaigns and the need for campaigns to maintain their autonomy and avoid the imposition of external agendas are further elaborated at the end of this chapter.

Table 29. Types, Examples, Sources, and Impacts of Resources

TYPE OF RESOURCE	EXAMPLE OF RESOURCE	SOURCE OR TYPE OF ACTOR/PROVIDER	IMPACT OF RESOURCE
Financial (material)	Money	Domestic and external	• Increased residents' participation in campaigns' actions • Sped up building and infrastructure activities • Helped spread nonviolent actions and popularize nonviolent resistance
	Selling food, T-shirts, and embroideries	Domestic and external	• Increased residents' participation
	Grants	Domestic and external	• Secured financial resources • Helped in building activists • Supported legal efforts
Building materials and equipment (material)	Bricks, cement, gravel, fuel, iron, sand	Domestic and external	• Increased residents' participation • Increased building and infrastructure activities
	Means of transportation (cars, buses), food and drinks, rooms, printing services	Domestic and external	• Increased number of participants in the campaigns' actions
In kind contributions (material)		Domestic	• Increased peoples' participation • Helped with transportation of material resources
Human and organizational (material)	Volunteer labor	Domestic	• Sped up building and infrastructure activities • Increased locals' participation
	Skills and experience in making hay-and-clay bricks	Domestic	• Maintained nonviolent campaigns • Sped up building and infrastructure activities
	Skills in solar panel installation	Domestic and external	• Made installation faster • Created sustainability
	Skills in building brick houses	Domestic	• Sped up building activities
	Skills in infrastructure projects	Domestic	• Sped up infrastructure activities
	Organizational networks	Domestic	• Maintained nonviolent campaigns • Fostered transparency and unity
	Skills in media communication and documentation	Domestic and external	• Secured financial resources • Helped advocacy and networking
Cultural (non-material)	Semi-Bedouin traditions	Domestic	• Fostered transparency and unity • Increased people's participation • Spread nonviolent actions
	Onah	Domestic	• Sped up building and infrastructure activities • Increased residents' participation
	Sumud	Domestic	• Increased residents' participation • Fostered transparency and unity
	Local knowledge	Domestic	• Sped up building and infrastructure activities • Protected material resources • Fostered transparency and unity
	Activists' experience and know-how	Domestic and external	• Increased people's participation • Fostered nonviolent discipline • Spread nonviolent resistance actions • Maintained campaigns
	Ma'dood	Domestic	• Secured financial support

Table 29, cont'd

TYPE OF RESOURCE	EXAMPLE OF RESOURCE	SOURCE OR TYPE OF ACTOR/PROVIDER	IMPACT OF RESOURCE
Social (non-material)	Family relations	Domestic	• Increased family members' participation • Maintained nonviolent campaigns • Fostered transparency and unity
	Neighborhood acquaintance	Domestic	• Maintained nonviolent campaigns • Increased residents' participation • Sped up building and infrastructure activities
	Communal trust	Domestic	• Increased people's participation • Fostered transparency and unity • Maintained the nonviolent campaigns

Increasing Residents' Participation and Ability to Organize Collective Actions

According to the survey and interviews conducted for this study, one of the most important impacts of material and non-material resources is the positive effect they have on residents' participation in nonviolent campaigns. The finding that they increase participation across age brackets and genders supports the assumptions made by social movement scholars (Zald 1992; Cress and Snow 1996; Edward and McCarthy 2004) that the availability of resources enhances collective actions. In Area C, the availability of material resources has meant that residents do not have to worry about transportation to campaign events, paying court fines, or covering the cost of bail in the event of their arrest.

Interviewees noted that the participation of residents in house construction increased when they learned that materials could be secured and made available for their campaign. They could see that their efforts would be productive, their actions would not be in vain, and they would contribute to solving their community's problems. In the Re-exist campaign in Al Mufaqara, many SHH residents participated in building houses once activists managed to secure the bricks and cement to build 15 homes in the community. Similarly, in the Bab Al Shams campaign, when activists knew that buses were made available to pick them up from different districts, participation levels increased. A youth activist explained that "when we managed to have solar panels in the Youth of Sumud campaign in SHH, more youth began joining us because at night we were organizing parties and it was easier to do it with electricity generated by the solar panels."[63]

The availability of building materials and equipment played a direct role in the number of buildings activists could erect and the number of roads, pipelines, or electricity supplies they could install to provide communities with infrastructure. Meanwhile, the availability of

---

63   Interview with a youth activist from SHH, 29 May 2019.

127

human resources and organizational structures enabled activists to do the work faster, while financial support helped activists buy material resources more easily. In-kind contributions facilitated communications and harnessed building materials. Non-material resources in the form of social and cultural assets also made it possible to mobilize more residents into the campaigns and garner more resources. For, example, activists recruited volunteers through family relations and semi-Bedouin traditions. In turn, these volunteers brought specific skills and experiences into the campaigns.

Fostering Activists' Nonviolent Discipline

Success in securing and managing material resources also increased participants' nonviolent discipline during their actions and transformed their resistance from an individual and often reactive response to collective and proactive initiatives. Activists realized that to garner local support they needed to develop campaign activities that directly addressed or solved the residents' real-life problems.

The use of violence against the Israeli army would do little to solve such problems; on the contrary, it would amplify them. It was obvious to campaign organizers that they needed to rely on nonviolent actions and maintain nonviolent discipline to protect themselves, their communities, their resources, and the results of their work—such as the buildings they had constructed.

Where nonviolent discipline was frail, this had a negative impact on the activists' work. For example, in the RV campaign, some new activists who lacked experience in nonviolent resistance started to throw stones at the settlers and soldiers. The army was able to leverage this violence to confiscate the mobile houses that had been constructed earlier.

The availability of human and financial resources in the form of lawyers providing *pro bono* services or money to pay bail and fines made activists less apprehensive about possible arrest and more willing to engage in nonviolent disruptive actions. When these resources are available, activists spend less time in jail than they otherwise would, and their speedy return to the local community helps to sustain nonviolent discipline. Furthermore, the availability of cameras to document activities creates evidence that makes the courts more likely to dismiss the army's claims that they faced violent disruptors. For activists, this also re-affirms the strategic value of remaining nonviolent.

Activists built the capacities of participants through workshops, training, and networking, which also created the opportunities to foster their commitment to nonviolent discipline. International solidarity groups also played an important part in encouraging nonviolent discipline. The PSCC established a capacity-building program with Al Quds University and the

University of Barcelona, with the help of Kurve Wustrow and Novact—two international organizations that help build both activists' capacity for nonviolent actions and networks to share information and experiences. The program also helped activists gain knowledge about activism in other contexts and understand success factors for other movements, including the importance of nonviolent discipline. This helped Palestinian activists strategize and design their own nonviolent campaigns suitable for their context. Furthermore, activists realized that international solidarity and allies would have been so much harder or even impossible to win over—and external material resources so much harder to secure and defend—had they not maintained nonviolent discipline during their campaigns.

Activists knew from their own experience that displays of violence would be a gift to the Israeli army, making it easier for the military to confiscate material resources and hurt people. Activists wanted to achieve their campaign goals with minimal harm to the participants and understood that this could only happen when nonviolent discipline was maintained. This allowed them to mute the physical power of the Israeli army. According to one of the activists, "If the goal of the action is to build a house or to cultivate the land, then doing it peacefully will enable us to do it. If we want to protect the available resources, then we have to be disciplined in nonviolent action."[64]

Activists have learned from experience that maintaining nonviolent discipline protects material resources that can then be used to meet the essential needs of communities. In addition, the resources acquired and protected by nonviolent actions further foster nonviolent discipline.

Enabling Activists to Organize Actions More Frequently

The availability of resources from activists' skillful acquisition and management increased the number of campaign actions that were possible. These resources enabled activists to organize more demonstrations and complete more infrastructure projects. During the RV campaign, the availability of money to pay for bussing volunteers allowed activists to organize frequent and creative actions. For example, after activists were evicted from Bab Al Shams, they reorganized and returned to the village in the form of a wedding procession. This creative nonviolent action misled the Israeli occupation forces but also reasserted the right of Palestinians to carry out the normal rituals of life in their own homeplace.

In the SHH and JVS campaigns, which ran over many years, activities were designed based on the availability of material resources. For example, in the early stages of the SHH campaign, activists used simple tools to renovate and expand caves and used tents to set

---

64   Interview with an activist from the north of the West Bank, 15 May 2019.

up homes for families. However, once they had secured building materials through the acquisition of grants, they would more frequently build permanent structures such as brick homes. Similarly, in the JV, local organizers began by renovating water wells, but once they secured financial resources they constructed water networks with plastic pipelines.

This positive pattern also applied to direct collective actions. Because of the acquisition of material resources, creative collective actions could be planned in all campaigns both proactively and more frequently. In the RV campaign, when the Israeli army tried repeatedly to evict activists from the village building sites, they returned to the sites multiple times a day in protest. This resilience, according to one organizer, created a need for transportation: "We tried to return to Ein Hejle five times in a day. Without the buses and cars that we provided to the participants we would have never been able to do that."[65] The acquisition of material resources augmented the capacity of activists in the SHH and the JV to carry out constructive resistance by establishing more infrastructure, including building roads, schools, and setting up renewable energy facilities.

Fostering Transparency, Unity, and Cohesive Relations Among Residents

Activists in the JV and the SHH who took part in the survey for this study emphasized that non-monetary resources such as building materials and in-kind contributions have had greater impact on internal unity than financial support, particularly as they were used to address the immediate needs of the community. Furthermore, they could be acquired and used without the skills necessary to develop and submit a grant proposal. They also did not depend on freedom to travel to cities where other materials would need to be purchased.

In contexts like the JV and SHH, residents and local activists often lack the knowledge and experience to prepare bids in response to funding calls and to conform to grant application criteria—which often insist that applicants have NGO status or a bank account. In situations like this, non-monetary resources—such as building materials, volunteer labor, and experience—become the easiest and most inclusive incentives for people to work together. Moreover, non-monetary resources and their results are more tangible to ordinary residents than financial support, and thus they foster transparency, unity, and cohesion between the residents. For example, providing a tent or bricks, cement, and sand for a family after their house is demolished is a more practical and appreciated form of support than a cash donation.

Before the establishment of PRNs such as the PSCC, local activists did not have the substantial financial and human resources needed to manage large grant projects. Donors

---

65   Interview with the coordinator of Ein Hejle from the center of the West Bank, 17 May 2019.

will not commit resources to organizations without administrative and reporting capacity—something that grassroots organizers usually lack. Therefore, activists prioritized acquisition of non-monetary materials from Palestinian actors because they would be used to increase the trust between activists and domestic and international providers externally and between activists and residents domestically.

Before the establishment of PRNs, activists did not have the substantial financial and human resources needed to manage large grant projects.

Resource administration can lead to fractures and disagreements, and while this might be of much less consequence for short-term campaigns, it is certain to derail attempts to organize in the long-term. Activists in the RV campaign did not believe that financial materials, non-monetary materials, and in-kind contributions had negatively affected their campaign's unity, but this was because the RV campaign was short-term and focused on discrete rather than continuous actions. Furthermore, its leadership had better organizational structures and skills than the SHH and JVS campaigns. Meanwhile, the SHH and JVS campaigns are long-term, running for 21 and 17 years-to-date respectively, and have thus been more vulnerable to fractures and disagreements.

The acquisition of resources and full community involvement are crucial if unity and transparency are to be achieved. Activists in the three campaigns organized face-to-face meetings and consulted the residents about the sources of the resources acquired for the campaigns' actions, using traditions and family relations to establish transparency. Activists avoided making individual decisions without the involvement of locals and heads of families regarding the solicitation and use of material resources. Through these relationships all committee members led and managed these resources. Non-material resources such as family relations and the semi-Bedouin traditions of *Onah* and *Sumud* fostered cohesive relationships between activists, enabling the effective cooperation among residents that allowed them to work toward unified goals. This approach helped the campaigns resolve disputes before they could escalate. In more positive cases, PRC activists prioritized local causes over their own self-interests and involved people in planning and decision-making through effective teamwork. One activist farmer from the north of the JV pointed out that "we are relatives and grew up to care about each other. The only way to be able to stay here and to counter the Israeli army is by working together."[66]

It is important to note that the long-term campaigns had cases of division, conflict, and rivalry resulting from the PRCs' and PRNs' acquisition, management, and use of material resources. This was made evident in the Sarura campaign in the SHH which started in 2017

_____

66   Interview with an activist from the north of the JV, 18 June 2019.

with activists rehabilitating caves to encourage people to return to live in the community. Activists recruited local volunteers and secured external financial support from Jewish Voice for Peace and other international solidarity movements. This financial support covered transportation, food, and logistics to allow activists to stay in the caves while they were rehabilitating them. A committee was formed from SHH activists, external Palestinian activists, and the resource providers, but individual personal relationships already existed between other SHH activists and the donors, and the committee failed to share with them the mechanisms they were employing to manage funds.

On other occasions, when external Palestinian activists intervened to direct the use of money without consulting the locals, this caused conflicts among the activists in the SHH. These conflicts culminated in the formation of another group called the Committee of Resilience and Defense, which saw activists withdraw from the Sarura campaign and start working elsewhere. Both groups—Youth of Sumud and the Committee of Resilience and Defense—have lost legitimacy in the eyes of most of the SHH residents, and few activists have continued to work in the original campaign.

In the JVS campaign, when some activists excluded the majority from managing money, this led to a misuse of funds and corruption. When pressure was put on the activists who were misusing the money, one of them left not only the campaign but the country.

Helping Mobilize and Popularize Nonviolent Campaigns in Various Areas

The acquisition of material resources by PRCs and PRNs has impacted the spread of nonviolent campaigns. The RV campaign was started in 2013 with the goal of expanding nonviolent resistance and connecting the village-level campaigns with the national struggle. Popular resistance had been limited in some villages to actions directed against the construction of the annexation wall, and activists sought to raise the profile of resistance. They were working to foster mass participation in their campaign to help the national cause end the Israeli occupation altogether. However, this type of mass mobilization depended on the availability of far more material resources than were usually required because the campaign involved rebuilding multiple villages. The coordinator of Bab Al Shams explained:

> When we started Bab Al Shams, we knew in advance that we needed more material resources. It is not like our campaign in Bil'in—my village—where the participants are from the village and after each action they go back to their homes. The RV campaign required all the planning and logistics we could muster to build a village from zero.[67]

---

67   Interview with the coordinator of Bab Al Shams, center of the West Bank, 7 May 2019.

One significant impact of material resources in the nonviolent campaigns was that they helped popularize the practice of nonviolent resistance across villages. Many villages outside the SHH were inspired by their campaign, particularly because it emerged in the wave of violence during the Second Intifada.

Villages were also inspired by the fact that the SHH campaign grew to encompass the right to education free of settlers' attacks. As one activist explained, settlers attacked students from Tuba village on their way to Al Tuwani school and prevented them from using the road that they had regularly used for years. Activists volunteered to accompany students on their way to and from school to protect them from settlers' attacks. The availability and the effective management and deployment of material resources—in this case, the volunteers—helped popularize resistance around the right to education, spreading nonviolent resistance across other communities as a result.

In the case of the SHH, the campaign spread to include all the communities in the area. This also happened in the JV as the JVS campaign spread from one community to another. Similarly, the RV campaign expanded to include many sites in Area C.

Maintaining the Independence of Campaigns to Avoid the Imposition of External Agendas

In all three campaigns, activists strove to generate material resources from domestic and external actors. In most cases, the availability of material resources had a positive impact on the campaigns. Yet, there were some concerns that receiving financial support from domestic and external actors produced a negative effect as discussed above in the "Fostering Transparency" section. One of the concerning aspects about the need for material resources is that there is a real danger of campaigns losing their autonomy and ceding control of their agendas to outside actors. Thus, this study found that it is crucial for the campaigns to maintain autonomy and avoid the imposition of external agendas.

The danger posed by the negative impact on campaigns that stems from the sources of material resources is a real one. Donations by domestic and international actors might come with the direct or indirect imposition of external agendas on the receiving party. This challenge was particularly visible when material resources were sourced from the PNA or from Palestinian political parties. There is no national unity among Palestinian factions, especially between Hamas and Fatah (the former is the prevailing power in the Gaza Strip while the latter is the dominant political force in the West Bank). Deep divisions between political parties that translate into lack of unity among the national liberation movements created significant challenges for activists. Securing material resources from either of the political factions could easily doom a campaign and expose it to criticism for having been co-opted by a specific political grouping.

Activists within the same committee can have allegiances to different Palestinian political parties. Also, the residents have varying levels of trust or distrust in the PNA. The organizers of the three campaigns therefore took the following steps to maintain the autonomy of their campaigns: First, they kept the campaigns independent from the PNA and the political parties, prioritizing the causes of their villages over any political affiliations. Second, activists represented their communities rather than their political parties. Third, they kept the leadership of the campaigns in the hands of activists who were themselves residents of the communities. Finally, they only accepted funds provided without conditions from the PNA.

Chapter 5 showed that there was involvement from a wide range of external actors from states to solidarity groups. The SHH and JVS campaigns communicated clearly and accurately with external actors. The international actors which have provided material resources to these community-focused campaigns have clearly understood the degree to which the rights of people in these communities have been violated, including their rights to housing, education, and the infrastructure vital for them to sustain a decent standard of living. This was achieved because of meetings between activists and international actors, as well as through induction meetings and clear procedures for implementing actions and holding workshops.

To avoid negative impacts resulting from ties with other organizations, activists in the SHH and the JV emphasized that, even if international actors supported their campaigns, this did not mean that they influenced or were involved in the design of campaign actions or their goals. The campaign did not accept conditional funds that might have tamed their plans. The SHH campaign stands as a model for the joint struggle in which Palestinian, Israeli, and international actors have worked together against the Israeli repression in Area C.

In the RV campaign, the PNA and the political parties provided material resources and participated in actions without taking a leading role, while the campaign leaders in Bab Al Shams and Ein Hejle managed to keep the control of the campaign in the hands of grassroots activists and away from political actors. The RV campaign actions gained the interest of the local media, and this, in turn, attracted the attention of the leaders of political parties and the PNA. However, grassroots activists, wary of undue political interference and political divisions spilling into the campaign, did not offer them any leadership roles. The grassroots activists kept the leadership of the campaign in their own hands and prioritized the campaign over their political affiliations.

The interviewees for this study highlighted disputes among the PRNs that had arisen due to the PNA providing financial support to the campaigns. For example, the financial support the PNA provided to the PSCC to support the RV campaign increased negative competition between the different PRNs, especially between the PSCC and the National Committee—the latter being viewed by the public as a Fatah committee. This competition arose because former PM Salam Fayyad financially supported the PSCC and not the National Committee. The National Committee, which was affiliated with Fatah, considered this move a challenge to the Fatah movement and so its members urged their followers to protest against Fayyad. As one of the activists drily commented, "If Salam Fayyad gave the money to Fatah,

The grassroots activists kept leadership in their own hands and prioritized the campaign over their political affiliations.

they would never be in conflict with him."[68] This had a negative impact on the RV and SHH campaigns to the extent that some of the Fatah activists stopped participating and tried to organize their own actions.

The PNA's financial support for the three campaigns created debate among activists. The majority of the activists interviewed for this study explained that it was a mistake to receive money from the PNA, whether it was given directly to the PRCs or processed through the PSCC. They argued that the PNA should support PRNs and PRCs with non-monetary materials through the local councils and with offers of legal defense, and they acknowledged the significant role played by the National Defense Committee when it volunteered their lawyers. The coordinator of the SHH campaign stressed that "the National Defense Committee provided us with the lawyers and helped us in opening a legal case against the eviction in 1999."[69]

The PNA's financial support, which started after 2009, has constrained popular resistance and limited activists' ability. The PNA's aim is to prevent a third intifada that might shake their power in the West Bank. Their involvement in popular resistance—particularly in light of its security coordination with the Israeli government and the absence of a national liberation strategy—is perceived by activists as interference by the Palestinian elites with negative consequences for the grassroots nonviolent resistance movement.

The PNA understands popular resistance within the institutional framework of the 1993 Oslo Accords, which means restricting resistance to low-impact activities such as sit-ins in city centers, to the detriment of nonviolent actions that directly challenge the occupation. The activists call this "controlled resistance" and, consequently, they regard PNA support as a form of co-option. They believe that "this is exploitation of the popular resistance" and has made the resistance movement too reliant on the PNA.[70] This dependence is made

---

68 Interview with the coordinator of the PSCC, center of the West Bank, 16 June 2019.

69 Interview with the coordinator of the SHH campaign, south of the West Bank, 1 May 2019.

70 Interview with an activist from the north of the West Bank, 19 May 2019.

evident by the fact that some of the grassroots activists now seek the PNA's consent for some of their actions. This form of co-optive power has also led many community members and activists to step back from the resistance, negatively affecting the level of participation in campaigns.

Some interviewees reported that PNA security forces have investigated them to find out who provides them with material resources. One activist mentioned, "When they investigated me, they claimed that I am importing external agendas, while in reality we are, in SHH, against agendas."[71] This tactic by the PNA is part of a growing trend that has seen attacks on activists increase.

However, other activists argue that the popular resistance has managed to influence the PNA's policy and strategy and has also produced material resources from the authority. As the co-founder of one of the PRNs explained:

> *Look at the period of Salam Fayyad. We were able to involve the government in all our actions and they never refused our demands. I think we managed to co-opt them, not the other way around. That is why the Fatah movement fights against the prime minister.*[72]

This research finds that the role of the political parties in the nonviolent campaigns was limited and lacking in strategy, and their participation was largely symbolic. In the best cases, Palestinian political parties occasionally offered transportation for their members but stopped short of urging them to participate in the movement. This was due to a lack of cohesion among the political parties.

Generally, there is low domestic trust in the Palestinian political elites. This study's interviewees reported their dissatisfaction with the role political parties have played in providing—or failing to provide—material resources. Campaign organizers factored in residents' concerns about the PNA and the political parties, and so they carefully managed their relationships with them. This helped them avoid the problems that arise when the political parties support their own followers in a partisan way, and it helped maintain unity in the SHH and JVS campaigns.

Sustaining Nonviolent Campaigns for More than Ten Years

The activists interviewed for this study agreed that the effective management and use of both internally generated and externally acquired material resources helped sustain

---

71   Interview with an activist from the south of the West Bank, 2 May 2019.

72   Interview with the co-founder of one of the PRNs, center of the West Bank, 7 May 2019.

nonviolent campaigns in Area C for long periods—since 1999 for the SHH campaign and since 2003 for the JVS campaign. Financial resources, along with human and organizational resources, have contributed to the campaigns' longevity.

The acquisition of financial resources—mainly grants from external actors but also money from the sale of goods and services—has helped the campaigns continue organizing nonviolent actions throughout this time. Acquiring grants accelerated the building of brick houses and installing of infrastructure in the SHH and the JV by allowing the activists to buy building and infrastructure materials. For example, after the PSCC secured grants from the French Consulate they bought building materials and managed to build more brick houses in the SHH. In the RV campaign, material resources made available by grants meant that activists were able to continue their building projects for close to two years, allowing them to complete the construction of eight villages.

Grants have also fostered the legal struggle, an important component sustaining the momentum of the campaigns. Money has been used to pay for fines, bail, and legal defense fees for arrested activists. Money has also been used to contest demolition orders in the Israeli courts. Thus, grants have helped protect activists, protect land, and postpone land annexation.

Other human resources sustaining the campaigns are the skills development of their participants. Activists have used their new skills in media communication and documentation to gain the attention and trust of external solidarity groups and established Palestinian NGOs, thus establishing viable domestic and international networks. This has grown advocacy efforts that increase the visibility of Palestinians' suffering and record their nonviolent response toward injustice. International solidarity groups disseminated the information they received from activists about campaign actions and became effective advocates on behalf of residents. Activists' documentation of their own activities encouraged international activists to make frequent visits to the campaigns on the ground to better understand the local situation. In return, this increased the availability of financial support to the campaigns, as was discussed in Chapter 5.

The skillful use of these resources also inhibited Israeli repression in some communities, causing the army's actions to backfire by increasing the visibility of Palestinians' suffering, highlighting their nonviolent discipline, and helping win international sympathy.

The constant presence of solidarity groups such as Operation Dove in the SHH—and their consistent support of communities with volunteers, funds, and skills for documenting the violations of residents' rights—helped sustain the campaigns. The fact that Israeli organizations such as Ta'ayush, Comet-ME, and B'Tselem were embraced by the campaign participants indicates the commitment of these solidarity groups to advocating, networking, and generating material resources for the SHH and JVS campaigns.

People in the SHH acknowledged that Israeli organizations have played a crucial role in their campaign's success. These organizations have also worked to expand the international solidarity network and connected the SHH campaign with other international actors who later provided additional material resources, such as money, volunteers, solar panels, and skills to maintain renewable energy. These international actors also provided training and capacity-building programs that targeted campaign members.

By harnessing the cooperation of international actors with certain privileges and access, activists have also been able to protect material resources while transporting them. Networking with international and Israeli groups—who are able to move on the settlers' roads with greater freedom and who are not subject to the same controls by the Israeli army—helped protect infrastructure materials.

The constant presence of external actors has not only helped protect material resources, it has helped protect people. For example, the Israeli group Ta'ayush accompanies shepherds and farmers in the SHH and the JV two days each week. Likewise, Operation Dove has been in the SHH since 2004, accompanying shepherds, school children, and farmers every day.

The effective acquisition, allocation, and use of materials resources have helped the SHH and JVS campaigns to achieve important goals and maintain momentum for two decades and has allowed RV campaign to continue building houses.

Key Findings and
Takeaways for Stakeholders

The Israeli historian Ilan Pappé has described the current Israeli occupation practices against Palestinians as ethnic cleansing (2006). The Palestinians living in Area C are facing forced displacement from their villages. Not only do they struggle for their rights to housing, access to their land, and infrastructure, but they also have to pressure the PNA to support their struggle to stay in their communities. Thus, Area C residents are the most marginalized and disadvantaged communities in the OPT.

Meanwhile, Palestinians are confronting occupation authorities that benefit from high levels of international support, particularly from the United States administration. The Trump plan released on January 28, 2020 is an example of an international arrangement that targets Palestinian communities living in Area C. Restrictions presently enforced on West Bank residents, combined with the lack of communication infrastructure, slow down activists and hinder their coalition-building with external allies who could help them acquire material resources. At a local level, Palestinians suffer from the lack of democracy, the lack of a coherent and coordinated liberation strategy, and divisions among Palestinian liberation movements.

This monograph has presented an in-depth empirical study of three nonviolent resistance campaigns in Area C of the West Bank: the SHH campaign, the JVS campaign, and the RV campaign. It has analyzed the types of material and non-material resources that specific nonviolent campaigns in the occupied territories have secured from domestic and external actors, and examined the mechanisms developed by the campaigns to manage and deploy them.

Several findings emerge that are relevant for constituencies engaged either directly or indirectly in nonviolent actions and organizing, for movements looking to acquire material resources from domestic and external sources to help their grassroots mobilization efforts, for allies who extend support to nonviolent campaigns and movements, and for those who conduct trainings or research in relation to nonviolent resistance, in general, or the Palestinian national struggle, specifically.

Takeaways for Campaign Organizers and Strategists in General

1. **Effective campaigns must have clear goals and prioritize the urgent needs of their communities.** The three campaigns analyzed here worked on rebuilding houses and organizing collective actions based on these needs. This approach helped activists maintain local legitimacy in the eyes of the residents of the SHH and the JV. The PRCs

focused on actions with clear and locally identified goals. This encouraged the mobilization of material resources, motivated residents to join the campaigns, strengthened internal coordination, and helped drive support from external actors.

2. **Activists should involve affected residents in the decision-making process when they assess the material resources needed for a campaign.** They should work closely with local people to conduct an organic needs assessment process. They can benefit from family relationships, face-to-face meetings, pre-existing organizations, and the skills of community members. This will help activists determine the nature and type of materials needed for a campaign. This monograph illuminates the strategies Palestinian activists adopted to determine which material resources were necessary in the absence of communication and networking facilities. It illustrates the importance of factors such as the clarity of campaign goals, the experience and know-how of activists and residents, the involvement of residents in the needs assessment process, and face-to-face meetings with residents and experts.

3. **Activists should rely on internal material and non-material resources—especially social capital, which helped residents secure the non-monetary materials needed to sustain long-term campaigns.** In the three campaigns, it has been easier for activists to internally generate non-monetary resources such as in-kind contributions and human resources rather than financial support (as shown in Table 7 on **page 18**), yet both monetary and non-monetary resources have had a positive impact on Palestinian participation. A reliance on internal material resources has also helped spread the practice of nonviolent resistance across other communities and has supported the momentum of campaigns, sustaining them for many years.

4. **Activists should leverage vivid events to mobilize internal and external material resources.** Dramatic events represent opportunities for oppressed people to advocate for their cause and gain media coverage, especially in the absence of communication skills and infrastructure. For example, despite communication challenges, the SHH campaign leveraged a dramatic event around the eviction of 15 communities in 1999 to generate material resources.

5. **Campaign organizers and strategists should see and use non-material resources such as cultural resources as a tactical opportunity—particularly in the case of rural isolated communities—to generate material resources from domestic and external actors.** Non-material resources helped Palestinian nonviolent campaigns to generate local volunteers and network with external actors who offered material resources. In the SHH, JVS, and RV campaigns, social and cultural resources helped mobilize material resources and increased participation.

6. **Activists can generate material resources by selling goods and services to visitors.** Palestinian activists generated money by selling homemade food and local products and by hosting visitors. This tactic increased local participation in their nonviolent campaigns, as happened in the SHH and JVS campaigns. Activists should manage the money generated from selling goods and providing services with transparency to avoid divisions among community members. They should also ensure that community members who provide these goods and services receive their fair earnings before a remaining portion of profits is given to help finance the campaigns.

7. **Campaign organizers should keep local grassroots activists in campaign leadership to prevent divisions among activists and to avoid co-option by national and international actors.** The case studies show that when leadership remained in the hands of local activists, participation from and unity among residents of local communities increased. Campaign organizers and strategists should strive to maintain the independence of their campaigns by not allowing external actors to co-opt their decision-making and needs assessment processes, especially when organizers solicit and accept material resources from external actors or where there is weak national unity among various movements and campaigns on the ground. The autonomous campaigns kept local activists in leadership roles and included affected communities in decision-making processes. Palestinian state actors such as the PNA and the political parties provided the campaigns with different material resources in a factionalist manner, often depending on the *ad hoc* decision of a prime minister rather than an articulate strategic choice. This, in turn, had a negative impact on the cohesion of the communities in Area C. The factionalism of material aid provision rapidly increased after a major split between Fatah and Hamas following the 2007 Hamas coup in Gaza.

8. **Activists should endeavor to secure material resources because their availability increases residents' participation in nonviolent campaigns, since participation becomes easier when people are offered things like transportation, training, and building materials.** Securing material resources can also strengthen activists' nonviolent discipline because the availability of resources covers lawyers' fees, fines, and bail, which keeps activists motivated. It can also help prevent the confiscation of materials, as shown in the three campaigns. The availability of material resources can help solve residents' problems—when they are offered building materials, for example—and can help activists overcome repression through training and sharing experiences. The research showed, through examples from Bab Al Shams and SHH, that the availability of material resources increased the residents' participation levels and their nonviolent discipline.

9. **Activists should manage and use material resources with transparency because this will lead to the sustenance of the nonviolent campaign and will help avoid disputes and divisions among activists.** Transparency among oppressed people and activists helps to maintain the momentum of a campaign and internal unity. Without transparency in decision-making, there can be disputes and divisions that can demobilize people and reduce participation. This study showed occasions when campaign organizers witnessed disputes and divisions resulting from a lack of transparency and trust, as well as occasions when activists adopted tactics that fostered transparency and trust to successfully maintain momentum and group unity.

Takeaways for External Actors in General and Those Working with Palestinians Specifically

1. **External actors should involve residents of affected communities in their decision-making and needs assessment processes.** This will help ensure that material resources are suitable to the needs, conditions, and circumstances of the people they aim to help. This also increases trust through open and participatory processes.

2. **External actors should pay attention to the messaging of domestic actors during and following dramatic events.** Domestic actors do not always have access to communication resources. Dramatic events create windows of opportunity for domestic actors' voices to be heard. Paying attention to their messaging in these periods can contribute to better-informed project design.

3. **External actors should allow domestic actors to determine the use of monetary resources that they supply.** External actors must ensure that their financial support does not become an instrument of co-option in their relationship with domestic actors. This can be achieved through the flexible and rapid distribution of small grants with few or no conditions.

4. **External actors can support domestic actors by providing opportunities for media coverage.** Media coverage allows local activists and organizers to increase local volunteer support and to secure material resources.

5. **External actors can support domestic actors by facilitating international travel to the affected region and by creating channels for the international sale of goods made by affected people.** This allows communities to generate funds for their campaigns from their own labor. It also allows workers to earn an income for their households, something which is often difficult to do in oppressed communities where there are few work opportunities—especially for women.

6. **External actors should respect the independence of domestic actors' organizations and campaigns.** Their partnerships with these groups should be executed in a

way that is sensitive to the nuances and complications that local groups could face domestically when interacting with external actors. These sensitively driven types of partnerships can result in the establishment of greater trust and more effective collaboration that benefits local campaigns and local communities.

Takeaways for Palestinian Communities and Residents

This research also offers lessons for the Palestinian communities living in Area C, which constitutes more than 60 percent of the Palestinian territory, with 10 percent of the West Bank population living under total Israeli military occupation.

1. **Palestinian communities should encourage, support, and even protect their local autonomy and actions independent of the political parties and the PNA in order to distance themselves from the distrust many Palestinians have toward these institutions.** This independence need not involve boycotting the political parties. Rather, Palestinian organizers must prioritize their campaign's cause over their ideological or party affiliations. This will help activists secure material resources, maintain unity, increase resident participation, and avoid being co-opted by local elites.

2. **Palestinian communities in Area C should generate internal material resources for their nonviolent campaigns.** Material resources garnered from internal, community-based sources have maintained the campaigns and helped them to acquire external material resources. Palestinian communities should favor securing non-monetary resources over financial support from internal and external actors. The case studies presented in this monograph have highlighted that the impact of resources depends both on the kinds of material offered and on the kinds of providers involved. Non-monetary materials have had broadly positive impacts on the campaigns, whether they were provided by external national actors or international actors. Meanwhile, financial support from external actors has sometimes had a negative impact on the unity of activists and has encouraged intervention from political elites trying to co-opt the popular resistance campaigns. However, small grants from solidarity groups have been more impactful than other forms of funding because the money provided was given without conditions, allowing activists to use it freely.

3. **Palestinian communities should reject external funding for projects if it means losing their autonomy, and they should establish systems of accountability and safekeeping to ensure no one has the opportunity to use external funding for personal gain.** Without proper mechanisms of accountability, external funding increases the potential for corruption among local activists. It can also overload them with administrative tasks. Moreover, external funding can create disputes and divisions between activists that lead to a loss of legitimacy in the eyes of the local population (Dudouet and Clark 2009; Roberts 2009; Chenoweth and Stephan 2011). On the other

hand, this study points to cases where specific forms of external financial support helped spread the practice of popular resistance, protect human rights, and build the capacity of activists and communities—for example, through small amounts of financial support provided by solidarity groups.

Takeaways for Scholars to Further Research on the Role of Resources in Nonviolent Campaigns

The research for this monograph was conducted in the context of an ongoing foreign occupation where the occupied people are living between the hammer of the occupation's repression and the anvil of divisions among the liberation movements. This monograph has explored how grassroots activists gained, secured, managed, and used material resources to help them wage sustained and successful campaigns in Area C in this complex situation, and it encourages scholars to think deeply and comprehensively about several issues:

1. **There is a need for more detailed understanding of the impacts on local campaigns under occupation when they receive material resources from domestic authorities in the absence of a liberation strategy and when the liberation movements suffer from internal divisions.** Further investigation is needed to explore the consequences of domestic political divisions for grassroots mobilization and campaigns. Such research should seek to identify practical lessons and solutions for campaign organizers, including strategies for avoiding co-option of campaigns by political factions, which can tame the campaigns' actions and lead to disunity among activists.

2. **The implications of the case studies and evidence gathered for this monograph indicate that, when campaigns have external support, the nature of the involvement of external actors and the kinds of material resources they supply can affect the momentum and outcome of a campaign.** Additional research is needed to better understand the connection between kinds of external actors and types of material resources, on the one hand, and the outcomes of nonviolent campaigns on the other (Martin 1993; Rigby 1995; Moser-Puangsuwan and Weber 2000; Carter et al. 2006; Clark 2009; Garton Ash 2009; Chenoweth and Stephan 2011; Dudouet 2011).

3. **More research is needed to focus on the role of traditional communities in harnessing material and non-material resources.** Attention should also be given to how the availability of communal cultural and social resources could be harnessed to acquire more necessary material resources from domestic and external actors.

4. **The relationship between the acquisition of material resources from anti-occupation Israeli groups and conflict transformation between Palestinians and**

Israelis also deserves further attention. This monograph found that Israeli activists and organizations have played a crucial role in providing material resources directly or through networking with other external actors. Future research could assess the extent to which Israeli groups, through the process of acquiring materials, facilitated the relationship between Palestinian activists and those groups, and to what degree nonviolent discipline resulted from the acquisition of material resources made available by the Israeli activists.

Appendix: The Interviews

In considering the three campaigns in Area C, this study incorporated the voices and experiences of Palestinian activists. Care was taken to ensure the inclusion of a range of campaign participants who could offer diverse insights into the role of material and non-material resources in the nonviolent campaigns. The interviewees also included a range of grassroots activists from PRCs and PRNs and volunteers from the campaigns.

A second key determinant of interviewee selection was the role of activists in the campaign and in the PRC in their local community in order to access a rich variety of viewpoints.

Gender was another crucial factor in the selection of interviewees. Women are playing an important role in the nonviolent campaigns, particularly in the effort to generate and protect material resources for the campaigns. The author interviewed 18 women from different geographical areas, and a snowball strategy was used to reach some of the interviewees in conservative communities. This was necessary due to some of the customs that prevail, especially in the rural villages.

The author conducted 41 interviews with activists from different backgrounds and geographical areas. The interviewees were drawn from different groups classified for the purpose of this study as:

Group One: The coordinators or co-founders of the PRNs—activists in the three campaigns with extensive experience in mobilizing materials and organizing campaigns. All of them have been jailed because of their involvement in the popular resistance movement and have been active in it for at least ten years. They are the advocates for the campaigns and liaise between the PRCs and the political parties, NGOs, and the PNA. Most importantly, they are from different political backgrounds and places. Interviews with different PRNs enabled the author to gather a wide range of opinions about the questions raised in this research, and this enriched the analysis of the research questions.

Group Two: The coordinators and members of the PRCs in the villages (some are also members of the PRNs). This group of grassroots activists are the active mobilizers of campaign participants, material resources, and coordination with the PRNs. They have been jailed for their involvement in popular resistance and people call them the "resistors of the wall" or "the expert activists." They are from the SHH and the JV and from villages across the OPT that are still organizing weekly demonstrations. This group comprises experts who move from one place to another, sharing their experiences with new villages and helping to spread popular resistance.

Group Three: Volunteer laborers, skilled professionals, and activist experts. This group is from the SHH and the JV but some of its members are from outside these communities. They are involved in the campaigns' needs assessment processes to determine the

146

necessary material resources, and they carry out the work of building houses and conduct direct actions. They volunteered their time and skills in the actions of the three campaigns.

Group Four: The residents of the SHH and the JV who participated in the nonviolent campaigns. They are also involved in everyday resistance in many ways. They were involved in the planning of the campaigns' actions but did not attend the PRC meetings in the SHH and the JV.

I adopted a uniform set of confidentiality measures that protect the identities of all interviewed activists. The names of the interviewees were coded for confidentiality (see Table 30). All the interviews were conducted only after verbal consent had been obtained from the interviewees.

Table 30. Interviewees, Coded for Confidentiality

CODE	GENDER	INTERVIEW DATE	PLACE	PROFILE
R1	M	1-May-19	SHH	The coordinator of the SHH campaign and a board member of the PSCC.
R2	M	20-May-19	SHH	The mayor of Al Tuwani. He is involved in generating material resources from the PNA.
R3	M	17-May-19	Central West Bank	The coordinator of the Bab Al Shams campaign. A former head of the board of one of the PRNs. He is one of the expert activists in the OPT and was jailed for 1.5 years for his involvement in the nonviolent campaigns.
R4	M	10-June-19	SHH	A committed labor volunteer who participated in campaign actions for more than 10 years. His house has been demolished and he was jailed for his involvement in housebuilding activities.
R5	F	10-June-19	SHH	An elderly woman from one of the hamlets of SHH. She was involved in facilitation and distribution of Oxfam materials.
R6	M	10-June-19	SHH	A youth activist from Tuba hamlet in the SHH. He is involved in the Sarura campaign.
R7	F	15-May-19	Central of West Bank	A woman activist who was involved in the RV campaign. She was arrested and shot in the leg because of her participation.
R8	M	18-June-19	JV	A volunteer laborer skilled in building water wells and renovating them. He is an expert in hiding materials to prevent the army from confiscating them.
R9	F	17-May-19	Central of West Bank	A woman activist involved in planning and organizing the Rebuilding Villages campaign. She was arrested more than once during the campaigns. She is a board member of one of the PRNs.
R10	F	18-May-19	North of the JV	A woman activist and the head of Fasayel village's women's center.
R11	M	18-May-19	JV	An activist expert in making hay-and-clay bricks.
R12	M	19-May 19	North of West Bank	An activist from the Rebuilding Villages campaign. Expert in organizing campaigns for more than 15 years, he was jailed for many years during the First Intifada and during the campaigns.
R13	M	05-May-19	SHH	The head of and activist in one of the hamlets in the SHH and the coordinator of the Re-exist campaign in Al Mufaqara campaign.
R14	F	18-June-19	North of JV	A woman activist who was hosting meetings in her tent and offering in-kind contributions.

R15	F	27-May-19	SHH	An elderly woman activist from Al Mufaqara Re-exist campaign. She witnessed the eviction of her community in 1999.
R16	M	6-June-19	JV	The coordinator of the JVS campaign with the responsibility of generating material resources.
R17	M	20-May-19	Central West Bank	The coordinator of one of the PRNs. He is an expert in networking and generating external material resources. He was jailed for his involvement in the campaigns.
R18	M	16-Jun-19	Central West Bank	The coordinator of the PSCC. He was involved in the three campaigns and networking with the PNA.
R19	M	5-May-19	SHH	An activist who has been involved in the SHH campaign since the beginning. He is an expert in generating internal material resources.
R20	F	7-May-19	SHH	A youth woman activist and the coordinator of the Sarura campaign. A member of the Youth of Sumud group.
R21	M	20-May-19	Central West Bank	One of the co-founders of a PRN, an expert in recruiting external material resources. He has a good network.
R22	F	04-June-19	North of West Bank	A woman activist involved in transporting material resources in the Rebuilding Villages campaign.
R23	F	24-June-19	SHH	A member of the SHH popular resistance committee. She was involved in building the school through generating internal material resources.
R24	F	24-June-19	SHH	A woman activist who was involved in protecting material resources in the SHH campaign.
R25	M	19-May-19	Central West Bank	The coordinator of one of the PRNs.
R26	F	29-April-19	JV	A woman activist lawyer who was following legal cases in the JVS campaign.
R27	F	29-April-19	JV	A woman activist involved in women's cooperatives and selling products.
R28	M	22-June-19	SHH	The coordinator of the Susya campaign. He has good relations with the Israeli activists.
R29	M	2-May-19	SHH	A youth activist from SHH involved in organizing direct collective actions.
R31	F	29-May-19	SHH	A woman activist involved in youth activities in the Sarura campaign.
R32	F	05-June-19	Central West Bank	A woman activist who was involved in the Rebuilding Villages campaign.
R33	M	07-June-19	JV	An activist who is an expert in making hay-and-clay bricks.
R34	M	30-April-19	JV	An activist who is an expert in transporting material resources in the JV area.
R35	F	2-June-19	SHH	A woman youth activist involved in organizing activities in the Sarura campaign.
R36	F	3-May-19	Central West Bank	A woman activist expert in needs assessment and the acquisition of material resources. She was involved in the SHH, JVS, and Rebuilding Villages campaigns.
R37	F	10-May-19	Central West Bank	A woman activist involved in providing food to the participants in the Rebuilding Villages campaign.
R38	M	19-May-19	SHH	A youth activist from the Sarura campaign and a member in the Youth of Sumud group. He is responsible for organizing cultural activities in the campaign.
R39	M	12-May-19	JV	A volunteer laborer expert in making hay-and-clay bricks.
R40	F	17-June-19	SHH	The head of Al Tuwani's women's cooperative and an active member of the SHH committee.
R41	M	10-June-19	SHH	The mayor of the SHH joint service council. His responsibility is to coordinate and network with the PNA ministries.

148

Cited Literature

B'Tselem. "Settlements." BTselem.org. 2019. **https://www.btselem.org/settlements** (accessed April 21, 2019).

Benford, Robert D., and David A. Snow. "Framing Processes and Social Movements: An Overview and Assessment." *Annual Review of Sociology* 26, no. 1 (August 2000): 611–639.

Bollack, Eloise. "6th Annual Festival of Non-Violence Resistance of the South Hebron Hills." *Al Mufaqarah R-Exist* (blog). June 24, 2013. **https://almufaqarah.wordpress. com/2013/06/24/6th-annual-festival-of-non-violence-resistance-of-the-south-hebron-hills/**.

Carter, April, Howard Clark, and Michael Randle. *People Power and Protest Since 1945: A Bibliography of Nonviolent Action.* London: Housmans Bookshop Ltd, 2006.

Chenoweth, Erica, and Maria J. Stephan. *Why Civil Resistance Works: The Strategic Logic of Nonviolent Conflict.* New York: Columbia University Press, 2011.

Clark, Howard. *People Power: Unarmed Resistance and Global Solidarity.* London: Pluto Press, 2009.

Cress, Daniel M., and David A. Snow. "Mobilization at the Margins: Resources, Benefactors, and the Viability of Homeless Social Movement Organizations." *American Sociological Review* 61, no. 6 (December 1996): 1089–1109.

Darweish, Marwan, and Andrew Rigby. *Popular Protest in Palestine: The Uncertain Future of Unarmed Resistance.* London: Pluto Press, 2015.

Dudouet, Véronique. "Nonviolent Resistance in Power Asymmetries." In *Advancing Conflict Transformation: The Berghof Handbook II*, edited by Beatrix Austin, Martina Fischer, and Hans J. Giessmann, 237–264. Opladen and Framington Hills: Barbara Budrich Publishers, 2011.

Dudouet, Véronique, and Howard Clark. *Nonviolent Civic Action in Support of Human Rights and Democracy.* Brussels: European Parliament, 2009.

Edwards, Bob, and John D. McCarthy. "Resources and Social Movement Mobilization." In *The Blackwell Companion to Social Movements*, edited by David A. Snow, Sarah A. Soule, and Hanspeter Kriesi, 116–152. Malden: Blackwell, 2004.

Gamson, William A., Bruce Fireman, and Steven Rytina. *Encounters with Unjust Authority.* Chicago: Dorsey Press, 1982.

Ganz, Marshall. "Resources and Resourcefulness: Strategic Capacity in the Unionization of Californian Agriculture, 1959–1966." *The American Journal of Sociology* 105, no. 4 (January 2000): 1003–1062.

Garton Ash, Timothy. "A Century of Civil Resistance: Some Lessons and Questions." In *Civil Resistance and Power Politics: The Experience of Non-Violent Action from Gandhi to the Present*, edited by Adam Roberts and Timothy Garton Ash. Oxford: Oxford University Press, 2009. 371–392.

Hutchison, Elizabeth D. "Spirituality, Religion, and Progressive Social Movements: Resources and Motivation for Social Change." *Journal of Religion & Spirituality in Social Work: Social Thought* 31, nos. 1–2 (March 2012): 105–127.

Isaac, Jad, Jane Hilal, Enas Bannourah, Nadine Sahouri, Elias Abu Mohor, and Khaldoun Rishmawi. *The Segregation Wall Impacts on Palestinian Environment.* Bethlehem: Applied Research Institute—Jerusalem (ARIJ), 2015. **http://intranet.arij.org/wordpress_arij/wp-content/uploads/2016/06/The_Segregation_Wall_impacts_on_Palestinian_Environment.pdf**.

Isaac, Jad. *Al Tuwani & Mosfaret Yatta Profile.* Bethlehem: Applied Research Institute–Jerusalem (ARIJ), 2009. **http://vprofile.arij.org/hebron/pdfs/At%20 Tuwani%20&%20Mosafaret_pro.pdf**.

Knoke, David. "Associations and Interest Groups." *Annual Review of Sociology* 12 (August 1986): 1–21.

Lahusen, Christian. *The Rhetoric of Moral Protest: Public Campaigns, Celebrity Endorsement and Political Mobilization.* Berlin: De Gruyter, 1996.

Martin, Brian. *Social Defence, Social Change.* London: Freedom Press, 1993.

McCarthy, John D., and Mayer N. Zald. "Resource Mobilization and Social Movements: A Partial Theory." *The American Journal of Sociology* 82, no. 6 (1977): 1212–1241.

Moser-Puangsuwan, Yeshua, and Thomas Weber. *Nonviolent Intervention Across Borders: A Recurrent Vision.* Hawaii: University of Hawaii Press, 2000.

Oberschall, Anthony. *Social Conflict and Social Movements.* New Jersey: Prentice Hall, 1973.

OCHA-oPt. *Life in a "Firing Zone": The Massafer Yatta Communities.* May 2013. **https://www.ochaopt.org/sites/default/ files/ocha_opt_massafer_yatta_case_ study_2013_05_23_english.pdf**.

OCHA-oPt. "Occupied West Bank Area C Map." Jerusalem: United Nations Office for the Coordination of Humanitarian Affairs, 2011.

Oliver, Pamela E., and Gerald Marwell. "Mobilizing Technologies for Collective Action." In *Frontiers in Social Movement Theory*, edited by Aldon D. Morris and Carol McClurg Mueller. New Haven: Yale University Press, 1992. 251–272.

Pappé, Ilan. *The Ethnic Cleansing of Palestine.* Oxford: Oneworld, 2006.

PCBS. *Preliminary Results of the Population, Housing and Establishments Census, 2017.* Ramallah: Palestinian Central Bureau of Statistics, 2018. **http://www.pcbs.gov.ps/portals/_pcbs/ PressRelease/Press_En_Preliminary_ Results_Report-en.pdf**.

Peace Now. *Settlements List.* Peacenow.org. il. 2018. **http://peacenow.org.il/en/settlements-watch/ israeli-settlements-at-the-west-bank-the-list** (accessed July 12, 2019).

Peace Now. *West Bank Population.* Peacenow. org.il. 2019. **https://peacenow.org.il/en/settlements- watch/settlements-data/population** (accessed July 12, 2019).

Popovic, Srdja, Andrej Milivojevic, and Slobodan Djinovic. *Nonviolent Struggle: 50 Crucial Points.* Belgrade: Centre for Applied Nonviolent Action and Strategies (CANVAS), 2006.

Richter-Devroe, Sophie. "Palestinian Women's Everyday Resistance: Between Normality and Normalisation." *Journal of International Women's Studies* 12, no. 2 (March 2011): 32–46.

Rigby, Andrew. "Unofficial Nonviolent Intervention: Examples from the Israeli–Palestinian Conflict." *Journal of Peace Research* 32, no. 4 (November 1995): 453–467.

Roberts, Adam. (2009). "Introduction." In *Civil Resistance and Power Politics*, edited by Adam Roberts and Timothy Garton Ash, 1–24. Oxford: Oxford University Press, 2009.

Ryan, Caitlin. "Everyday Resilience as Resistance: Palestinian Women Practicing *Sumud.*" *International Political Sociology* 9, no. 4 (December 2015): 299–315.

Shbaita, Rima. *Towards Policies to Promote Development in Area C.* Ramallah: Masarat, 2018. **https://www.masarat.ps/article/4793/-edn**.

Soliman, Mahmoud. *Mobilization and Demobilization of the Palestinian Society: Towards Popular Nonviolent Resistance from 2004–2014.* Unpublished Doctoral Dissertation. Coventry: Coventry University, 2019.

Teeffelen, Toine van. *Sumud: The Soul of the Palestinian People.* Bethlehem: Arab Educational Institute, 2011.

United Nations. *Declaration of Principles on Interim Self-Government Arrangements.* New York: United Nations General Assembly, 1993. **https://peacemaker.un.org/israelopt-osloaccord93**.

United Nations. *Call for Ceasefire and Just Solution in the Middle East,* Resolution 338. New York: UN Security Council, 1973. **https://peacemaker.un.org/middleeast-resolution338**.

United Nations. *Decisions on the Middle East,* Resolution 242. New York: UN Security Council, 1967. **https://peacemaker.un.org/middle-east-resolution242**.

Verba, Sydney, Kay Lehman Schlozman, and Henry E. Brady. *Voice and Equality: Civic Voluntarism in American Politics.* Cambridge, MA: Harvard University Press, 1995.

White House. *Peace for Prosperity; A Vision to Improve the Lives of the Palestinian and Israeli People.* Washington: White House, 2020. **https://trumpwhitehouse.archives.gov/wp-content/uploads/2020/01/Peace-to-Prosperity-0120.pdf**.

Zald, Mayer N. "Looking Backward to Look Forward: Reflections on the Past and Future of the Resource Mobilization Program." In *Frontiers in Social Movement Theory*, edited by Aldon D. Morris and Carol McClurg Mueller, 326–348. New Haven: Yale University Press, 1992.

Zald, Mayer N., and David Jacobs. "Compliance/Incentive Classifications of Organizations: Underlying Dimensions." *Administration and Society* 9, no. 4 (1978): 403–424.

About the Author

Mahmoud Soliman is a Palestinian nonviolent activist and academic. He has more than 15 years of experience in organizing nonviolent campaigns and nonviolent collective actions against building the Segregation Wall and the Israeli illegal settlements in occupied Palestine. He is one of the founders of Palestinian nonviolent grassroots networks and the co-founder of the popular nonviolent resistance committees in occupied Palestine. He completed his PhD in Peace and Conflict Resolution Studies with a focus on mobilization of Palestinian society towards nonviolent resistance in the period from 2004 to 2014.

Acknowledgments

It has only been possible for me to conduct this research due to the support and encouragement from the ICNC team, especially Maciej Bartkowski. I am truly grateful for their support.

I would like to offer my appreciation to all the Palestinian activists who engaged in this research in Occupied Palestine. They gave me their time and opened their minds and hearts to answer the research questions and to give me their feedback for the findings of the research. A deep thanks to the people who helped me in translations and offered me technical assistance. I would like to express my deepest thanks to the residents of the Palestinian marginalized communities for their generous hospitality and their cooperation during the conducting of this research.

www.ingramcontent.com/pod-product-compliance
Lightning Source LLC
Chambersburg PA
CBHW042345030426

42335CB00030B/3464